Do you w ....
Meditate?

Do you want to
Meditate?

Eric Harrison

DO YOU WANT TO MEDITATE?

Published by Perth Meditation Centre, Western Australia
Earlier editions published 1991,1993 and 1998
© Eric Harrison 2002

Perth Meditation Centre offers:

Four terms of courses each year

Workshops

Seminars

Corporate programs

Private consultations

Correspondence courses

PMC sells books by Eric Harrison:

Do You Want to Meditate?

The Naked Buddha

Why Meditation is good for your Health

and the 3-CD set:

How to Meditate

For further information

see the back pages of this book, or contact:

Perth Meditation Centre

P O Box 1019, Subiaco WA 6904, Australia

Ph (08) 9381 4877

www.perthmeditationcentre.com.au

Contents

Introduction

Meditation is a delightful and healthy thing to do. It brings out our natural instinct for stillness and mental clarity. By meditating, we relearn a skill often lost since childhood: the ability to relax at will and return to inner balance. We find out who we are and what we feel, and how to act intelligently in a less-than-intelligent world. Personally, I can't imagine anything more valuable.

Meditation has been at the centre of my life for over thirty years now. Since 1987, I've also been teaching it as my full-time occupation, though this doesn't stop people from asking me if I have a *real* job as well.

When I started to teach I faced two difficulties. First, meditation is such a simple skill that it's difficult to convince adults that it's worth doing. (Little kids usually get it immediately). Meditation is the art of simplifying and focusing our mental activity, and it can seem too elementary.

Secondly, although meditation is found worldwide, it invariably takes the flavour of its local culture. Since it's been most fully developed in India, it usually comes with Buddhist or Hindu ideas and traditions that don't always travel well in the West. It's not easy to extract the essence from its culture. Nonetheless, this is what I've tried to do, ever since I started teaching.

Like many Western teachers, I was trained in a Buddhist context which inevitably mixed the practical exercises with traditional beliefs and customs. I decided, however, to teach only what I was sure really worked. After years of sifting, I found that the meditation practices became ever more beautiful and useful, but the Buddhism gradually faded away. I'd found the gold in the bottom of the pan.

So this book presents *just* meditation. No Buddhism, no beliefs, no positive thinking, no magical cures, no moral guidelines, no promises, no formal spirituality. Instead, this book is an invitation to become very good at relaxing the body and calming the mind. It is my conviction that all good things arise from this. They certainly have for me, and I hope they will for you.

MY BACKGROUND

Full-time Western meditation teachers like myself who are not monks or nuns are very rare. However, we do exist and I met my peers at three conferences in California in the 1990s. On that evidence, you can say we are typically in our forties or fifties (because it takes that long to get a handle on the mind). Most of us spent years on the hippie trail in Asia from the early '70s, and/or trained in a Buddhist or Hindu tradition. And, in contrast to the East, there are almost as many female as male teachers.

I was born in New Zealand in 1949. I studied literature at university, but read more extensively in psychology and philosophy. After graduating at 20, I traveled through Asia for three or four years, encountering mind-expanding drugs on the way.

At that time, I became a self-taught meditator. At first I just meditated to settle down when my mind was going wild. If I was at a party, I would sit in a corner and focus on my breathing. Then I used meditation to deliberately enjoy the beauty of my surroundings. When I was in Bali or India or the Himalayas, I wanted to really be there. Finally, I found it helped me get my mind clear when I had to make important decisions. At that time, I used meditation as a useful occasional skill.

I started formal training in 1975, doing 10-day retreats in the Burmese tradition. The first one I attended had a stunning effect on me. I knew I'd found my passion in life. I was seriously tempted to drop everything and wholeheartedly pursue meditation.

I persuaded myself that leading a more balanced life was better, but I now think that was the worst decision I've ever made. It was not until 1983 that I started three years training with Western teachers in the Kagyu lineage of Tibetan Buddhism.

This resulted in a seven-month retreat in the South Island of New Zealand. For most of that time, I lived in a tiny unheated hut high on a mountainside in the Southern Alps. I saw no one all week, except for Wednesdays, when I would collect my next week's food and spend the night with my girlfriend in the adjacent hut.

At last I had the solitude and stillness I'd always craved. I sat (i.e. meditated) for about nine hours a day, starting about 3 am. I also did two hours of yoga, two hours walking, a little writing and reading, and the housekeeping. I could feel the old self dying and a new one emerging. It was an unstoppable process and all I had to do was watch.

They were the richest months of my life. Nothing has matched them since. Despite the inner dramas and occasional horrible patches, I was not bored for a minute. I found my mind was profoundly interesting and intelligent if I stopped trying to manipulate it. I seemed to be a natural hermit.

I considered becoming a monk and spending years in solitude. It was the obvious thing to do, but I would have felt a hypocrite if I had. I just couldn't see my affection for the opposite sex as an obstacle to be overcome. I felt there must be a better way of integrating the inner and outer parts of my life.

I left my little hut when the winter really set in. The hut had huge windows and no insulation. When the first snowfalls came, it was freezing. After several days wearing all the clothing I owned, and often my sleeping bag as well, I knew I had to go.

Reluctantly, I returned to my little farm in the sunny north. I was part of the 'back-to-the-land' movement of the 1970s. For eight years I had built houses, tended bees, planted trees, grown fruit and vegetables and helped my friends do the same.

After my long retreat, that lifestyle no longer appealed to me. My teachers had said I now knew enough to teach meditation. There were few possibilities in New Zealand, so on my thirty-sixth birthday, I returned to Australia and eventually settled in Perth.

HOW I BECAME A TEACHER

My teaching career started very modestly with a free course to five people in a local 'learning centre'. We could hear the children in the creche and people gossiping in the corridors as we tried to meditate. This is what we euphemistically call 'meditation in daily life'.

However, I seemed to be in the right place at the right time. Perth was ready for a non-religious meditation teacher, and my work grew rapidly. Initially I taught at civic centers, universities, schools, government offices, prisons and from my home. The surroundings were rarely satisfactory so, in 1990, I opened up the Perth Meditation Centre and persuaded people to come to me. Soon I was teaching about 1000 people a year.

The Centre was in West Perth, just a mile from the heart of the city. It overlooked Kings Park, 400 acres of magnificent bush land with escarpment views over the Swan River. People coming to classes would go up two flights of stairs, past the offices of Fairfax Newspapers and the Mineral Mapping Agency. The centre itself occupied the whole top floor and was simply furnished, with jungles of vegetation in each corner.

The main teaching room was an unusually beautiful space to find in office-land. It was spacious and airy, with light and sky views coming through windows on three sides. It was very suitable for a class of twenty, though at times we squeezed in over a hundred people for talks and workshops.

I had descended from the mountains of New Zealand to the marketplace in Perth. Without consciously planning it, I realized this had always been my goal. Much as I loved my time in retreat, I found it too easy, being a natural introvert. For me, it was a greater challenge to find a useful role in the outer world.

Similarly I didn't want my students to feel that they had to escape to the mountains to meditate. After a week or two of classes, they found themselves meditating well in an office block in a busy part of town. They gradually learnt to do the same at home, amid the sounds of traffic outside and the TV down the hall.

In the mid 1990s, I was employing two other teachers and a secretary and still working 70 hours a week. My overheads were $100,000 a year. Then one of my wealthy students said to me, "With those overheads, no small businessman like you can sleep well at night." And he was right. I wasn't a good model for my students.

When the building was demolished in 1998, I laid off my staff. I reduced my classes by a third and my overheads by half. I moved to the cafe district of nearby Subiaco. Coincidentally, my new premises have exactly the same dimensions as my old ones. I took up golf and gave myself more time to think.

The result was that I wrote more books. This book is in fact the fifth revision of a 48-page booklet that first came out in 1989. I hope it will be my last word on meditation for beginners. I have too many other books to write to revise it again soon.

In 1999, I wrote a book on meditation and health, in response to the many people who come to me for health reasons. The latest edition of that, entitled 'Why Meditation is Good for your Health', is due out in April 2003. One or other of these two books is now published in nine countries and seven languages.

I've always taught in the corporate world, but the demand has increased in recent years. In particular, I train people to relax in short bursts during the working day. A highlight this year was eight days teaching on the oil rigs off the coast of Karratha. I've also trained some 30 people recently to be able to teach meditation in their own work or homes.

SAYING GOODBYE TO BUDDHISM

Like many Western teachers, I had an uneasy relationship with the Buddhist tradition I trained in. I loved its psychological insight and brilliant meditation practices, but was very aware of its faults. Values I took for granted as a child of the '60s' - equal rights, respect for the individual, caring for the planet, rational enquiry, even democracy - are alien to Buddhism, which remains an old-time religion at heart. So I still pursued my interests in Western psychology and philosophy.

Yet I felt an obligation to Buddhism and wanted to pay it back. At the very least, it had led me to a wonderful livelihood. So I tried to be a modernizing influence within the various Buddhist groups with which I was involved.

I sponsored the visits to Perth of non-monastic Western men and women from the Tibetan, Burmese and Zen traditions. I gave workshops and lecture series on Buddhist themes. I wrote my book, *'The Naked Buddha - a demythologised Account of the Man and his Teaching'*. I exposed thousands to their first taste of Buddhism.

After a decade of this I had to face the truth. My attempts to bring Buddhism to people, and to bring Buddhism into the 20th century, had borne small fruit. For every person who liked it, a hundred found it unappealing, and I gradually understood why. Buddhism has great strengths, but many flaws as well. It was time to leave it behind.

My passion for meditation had taken me far into Buddhism, but my roots in Western culture go deeper. It seems that my first allegiance is to Socrates and the Western tradition of sceptical enquiry. I'll never feel at home with a religion.

WHY PEOPLE MEDITATE

I found that teaching meditation was an excellent discipline for me. It forced me to analyse what happens in meditation so I could explain it to others, and this helped my own practice enormously. Though meditation is a non-verbal state, it is still useful to examine it and figure out how it works. It can often be explained in terms of mental and physical processes that any psychologist or doctor would feel comfortable with. I've always wanted my students to understand exactly what they were doing.

I particularly like to see students use meditation for their own purposes. I tell them that meditation is just a vehicle. It's up to them where they drive it. I don't think anyone has become enlightened under my direction, but I am very happy when I see them achieve what they want.

Over the years, I've seen thousands of people get profound results from meditation. The research literature say that meditation helps with insomnia, migraines, hypertension, digestive and respiratory problems, chronic pain, immune function and anxiety. These are just the most obvious benefits and I've seen them all.

I see people who dramatically lower their bloodpressure; who vastly improve their sleep or their digestion; who stop having migraines or panic attacks; who cut down their medication or avoid the need for surgery. Others find meditation invaluable in coping with invasive medical treatment or the trauma of chronic illness; or in managing overwhelming pressures in their work or private life.

I see the insomniac who gets her first full nights' sleep in years; the person in severe pain who can reduce his morphine intake by two-thirds; the agoraphobic who can take her child to the park again; the elderly man who survives a six-year legal battle in better health than when he started; the women who succeed in getting pregnant after years of trying; the mothers-to-be who manage the birth process well; the men who regain sexual function; the people who recover from breakdowns or post-traumatic stress disorders; the performers and sportspeople and students who attain their best with the help of meditation.

Yet meditation is much more than just an antidote to stress. People fall in love with meditation for the way it enriches their life. They often find a degree of peace and tranquillity they never imagined possible. They relish the enhanced sensory awareness and appreciation of beauty that meditation brings. They find it gives them a mental clarity and a subtlety of perspective that is delightful in itself. They find it easier to make good decisions, and the complexities of life become less complex.

For many, meditation opens the door to a rich inner life. There is much beauty just below the surface of our everyday mind. People start to hear their inner voices, and find out who they really are. Paradoxically, this also helps their outer life. Being at ease with themselves, they also feel more empathy towards others. They find a healthier balance and more depth in the many activities of their lives.

They frequently move into therapy or analysis or creative expression, or into yoga or other forms of spiritual activity with increased confidence. Many people feel their lives are lacking something, or that they've lost contact with their souls on the way. If you are one of these, then meditation can help you find your soul again.

As far as I can tell, most of these positive results come from being more relaxed and mentally clear. I also see that achieving this is not complicated at all. I've found that meditation easy to teach and easy for people to learn. It simply requires some understanding and the discipline to practise. I hope you get as much satisfaction from it as I have.

Eric Harrison, 2001
Perth, Western Australia
www.perthmeditationcentre.com.au

Chapter one

How to use this book

DO YOU WANT TO MEDITATE?

The book presents all the instructions I give in my basic course in Perth. I've designed it especially for people who are keen to learn but who are unable to attend my courses. It's a ready-made kit. You just add time. If you read this book, you will know what meditation is and how to do it. If you invest fifteen minutes a day for the next month or two, you can learn a skill that bears fruit for the rest of your life.

First, it might help to know how I usually teach. I run 60 or 70 courses a year, mostly of 7 weeks duration. The average class has 15 people, sitting in a circle of chairs, and runs for an hour and a half.

I first introduce a particular meditation, much as I do in the following chapters. I then guide people through the meditation for 20 minutes or so. Then we discuss it afterwards, so people don't just have the experience: they also understand what they are doing. We usually do two or three meditations each class, and revise the major ones periodically. The students select the particular practices they like and work with those.

The students find it easy to meditate in class, but then they face the hard bit. They have to find the time and place to practise, and do it often enough for satisfaction. This will be your biggest challenge, too.

There are many ways you could use this book. You may simply read it to understand what it's all about. If you already know how to meditate, you can pick out useful ideas to enhance your practice.

If you actually teach meditation yourself, or would like to do so, this book can be a resource or give you a structure to work on. But if you feel you really want or need to learn it properly, I suggest you do the following.

CHOOSE YOUR MEDITATION

First, read this book with big pauses. Read the instructions for any exercise two or three times, then put the book down and do it. Try out as many exercises as you like while you read.

After you've read the book through, choose a favourite exercise and practise it several times. You need to do a meditation at least four times over four days for it to go into long term memory. Realise that some practices are more useful and fundamental than others. Your favourite is likely to be one you will meet in the first few chapters.

Scattered through the book are dozens of 'spot-meditations'. You can do these whenever an opportunity arises - at traffic lights, in queues, while walking or doing housework. These are not designed to take you to the point of sleep. They just strip off the top 20% of tension and slow down the mental chatter. These are the most time-efficient practices.

FIND YOUR TIME AND PLACE

Most people fail to learn because they can't find the time ('too busy') or the place ('too noisy'). Or they don't want to try unless they feel in the right mood. Even if you know how to meditate, this is your first big challenge. You can't expect a half hour space to suddenly open before you. You have to find it.

Even if your week seems insanely busy, keep this question in mind: "When could I meditate?" or "Could I meditate right now?" If you ask the question repeatedly, you start to find little gaps during the day. If you can at least do a spot-meditation or two, these have a tendency to stretch into longer ones. More about this later.

GOOD PREPARATION

Do 20- or 30-minute meditations under good conditions whenever you can. It's easiest to go to a class or a group, but you can be very comfortable at home. Make sure you're not going to be interrupted. Put soft music in the background if you wish. Re-read the instructions for the meditation you are going to do before you start, and check your results afterwards.

USING THE CD SET, 'HOW TO MEDITATE'

I've recorded eight of the meditations in this book on to CDs. The 3 CD set contains two and half hours of guided meditations with light musical accompaniment. In my classes, I talk people through the meditations till they get the hang of it. Eventually, they internalise the instructions and don't need me any longer. Using the CDs will duplicate this method. It is by far the easiest way for you to learn how to meditate.

You can also do a 'long distance course' with me or one of my assistants, by email, phone or post. Using the CDs as a format, one of us will guide you week by week in establishing your practice and helping you manage the difficulties. See the website or the back of this book for details.

IMPROVING YOUR PRACTICE

It seems that half the Australian population has 'done a bit of meditation' at some time or another! Many people 'sort of' know how to do it. Their problem is that they often don't know what they're doing, or how it works, or what they are trying to achieve.

If you're one of the above, you can use this book as a study manual. I'll encourage you to get a good intellectual understanding of the subject. You should be able to look back on a session and notice what worked and what didn't, and what you can do to improve it.

So please experiment and find out what works for you. There is no one correct experience. All good meditators develop their own individual style in time, even if they seem to be doing the same thing on the surface. If you understand the basic principles - 'be present, focus and watch' - you can adapt them in an amazing variety of ways.

TEACHING OTHERS

In recent years, I've trained 30 people as meditation teachers. I also train people by correspondence. If you're a meditator of a few years standing and you have good people skills, you may be quite capable of teaching others.

Simple as meditation is, I find that every teacher has a individual approach. Hardly anyone teaches meditation as a pure skill, the way I do. It's usually combined with disciplines like health care, yoga, bodywork, reiki, counselling, spirituality, corporate training and so on. Meditation has much to offer all of these.

It is easy to be a meditation 'leader'. Most people will only meditate when someone leads them through it anyway. A 'leader' is quite different from a 'teacher', who trains people to meditate independent of any supports. Yet even the role of meditation leader requires strong personal ethics and self-awareness. It's prone to subtle manipulations on both sides.

If you're teaching meditation, you are welcome to use this book (or the CDs) to give you a course structure. I am happy for this material to be used as notes, but as a courtesy, I would like to be acknowledged if you do this. Meditation is usually a very positive thing to share with others, and I will encourage you in that.

HOW YOU BECOME A GOOD MEDITATOR

If you read this book, you might assume you understand what is said here, even if you haven't meditated before. In fact, my students commonly say it takes a year or two before they really understand the meaning of a certain instruction. These instructions, though simple, have depth. It's good to read this book right through a few times while you practise to really get it.

You're also likely to make another mistake. Because the skill is simple, you might assume you can do it. It just doesn't work that way. You only get good at a skill by practicing it regularly, no matter how simple it seems. I frequently meet doctors, psychologists and group facilitators who use meditation exercises in their profession without actually doing it themselves. They know how. They can tell others. They just don't do it themselves, and so there's something missing in their understanding.

Assuming you are well trained, whether you succeed or fail is largely a matter of the time you give it. If you put in the hours, you'll succeed. Otherwise, you'll be disappointed. This is one of those eternal laws you can't get around. I'll be very happy if you learn to meditate from this book, and make the skill your own. Good luck.

Chapter two

Relaxation and Clarity of Mind

Meditation is about relaxing the body and calming the mind. These two aspects support each other. If you relax physically, you are better able to break the grip of your thoughts and observe them dispassionately.

This awareness, or clarity of mind, depends on some degree of stillness. Meditation is about finding that calm, tranquil place that gives the mind freedom. In other words, relaxation is the foundation for clarity of mind.

Of course, it's not easy to be still and present, even for a minute or two. We much prefer to live in our stories and fantasies about the past and future. This is an eternally restless activity, full of promise and frustrations, but if we want a calm clear mind, we have to let it go. The first stage is learning to consciously relax the body.

RELAXATION AND AWARENESS ARE THE KEYS

We can define meditation as 'any technique that relaxes the body and calms the mind', yet it can seem much more complicated than that. People variously meditate to relax, to heal cancer, to get rich, to find their inner self, to play better sport, to see God, or to fall asleep! It also comes in many flavours - Hindu, Buddhist, Christian and

New Age - and frequently promises the earth. Furthermore, some practices are good, some useless, and many are linked with cults.

But if you regard meditation as a technique rather than a goal, it all makes sense. It is the vehicle, not the destination. Once you learn how to drive, you can go where you like, and pretty much drive any car as well. Like the skill of driving, most techniques are very similar below the surface. You could almost say it is one technique expressed in a thousand different ways.

When scientists analyse a medicinal herb, they try to isolate the active ingredient in it. In meditation, the active ingredients are physical calm and clarity of mind. These are the things that actually work beneath all the glamour and hype of specific practices. Without them, nothing much happens.

People often tell me, "I've tried meditation, but I don't get much out of it." When they sit, they relax a little, they slow the mind a little and then day-dream or fantasise or fall asleep. Consequently, they get mediocre results despite their high aspirations.

It's all about looking after the basics. After 30 years of meditating, I know what works: quality relaxation and awareness. Everything starts here. Many beautiful things can happen when you meditate, but not without the spade work.

If you like the idea of having a calm, clear mind, this is probably the book for you. I don't talk much about visionary states or miracle cures or spiritual matters. I just want you to understand the basics. They are worth getting right. So let's look at what relaxation and clarity of mind actually are.

WE ALL RELAX

Relaxation is a natural biological process. It is that function of the nervous system that winds us down towards sleep. The nervous system works like a thermostat. One part winds us up. We can call this 'the stress response'. The other part winds us down. We can call it 'the relaxation response.' These two responses alternate during the day, as our energy goes up and down. At night, the relaxation response takes over completely.

Some people say they never relax, but of course they do. Everyone gets too tired to keep going and they fall asleep eventually. That's what the relaxation response does. If we didn't relax at all, we'd burn out and be dead in a few days.

What those people mean is that they always feel tense, and they can't consciously relax. For these people, meditation is about being able to switch on the relaxation response deliberately. We all have that switch in the mind, tucked away in the hypothalamus. We just have to find it. Meditation is about quickly and consciously relaxing, whenever we want to.

DEEP RELAXATION

It is useful to think about relaxation in two ways. First, we can think of it as 'deep relaxation', or as a state close to sleep. In a long meditation, you often hover in a place where you are not quite asleep or awake. In fact you are balancing between the two. Since the body often feels like it's gone to sleep, we can call it the 'body asleep, mind awake' state.

We all know this sleep threshold state, since we pass through it at least twice a night. It is quite lovely, and I'll talk about it in more detail later. Meditation enables you get there quickly and to stay alert while you're there.

In this state, all the biological systems in the body are returning to balance. The muscles soften, the racing heart slows down, the digestive system starts working again, and so on. The body is repairing and balancing itself. Furthermore, it instinctively feels good, which is why we do it. Because you're burning very little energy, it is called a state of 'homeostasis' or rest.

HAVING A RELAXING DAY: BEING IN BALANCE

We also talk about relaxation in another way. We'll say, "I had a relaxing day", or a "good day". This doesn't mean you were at the point of sleep all day. It means you were cruising along, pacing yourself well and enjoying what you were doing. You weren't stressed out or flustered, even though you might have been quite active.

This is called a state of 'allostatic balance'. I also call it 'cruising'. It is when you are using just the right amount of energy for whatever you are doing. Your energy expenditure will go up and down during the day, but it won't ever be excessive.

Usually when you are in balance, you are just doing what you are doing, and not thinking about much else. In other words, you are in the present. For example, if you walk through a park, and simply enjoy the sights, sounds and sensations of the walk, you'll feel relaxed and enjoy yourself. If however, you also worry about work or your family while you walk, you'll be tense and burn more energy as a result.

Sometimes we're relaxed or in balance throughout the whole day. At other times we go up into the 'stress zone'. Some people are in the stress zone all day, which is quite painful and bad for their health. This is what makes for a 'bad' or 'difficult' day.

TENSION AS A HIGH ENERGY STATE

We can think of tension as a state where you burn energy fast, and relaxation as the opposite. Tension is actually the 'fight-or-flight' response, mobilising a lot of energy so you can run away or beat someone up. In other words, your 'metabolic rate' is high. Deep sleep, on the other hand, is where you burn the least energy and the body repairs itself in preparation for the next day. In this state, your metabolic rate is low.

We can also think of the tension-relaxation cycle as having several settings, like the volume control on a stereo. From maximum to minimum these go something like this: 'panic, stress, balance, relaxation, sleep'.

You don't have to go to deep relaxation or sleep to improve your quality of life. If you suffer a panic attack, it's a great relief to go from 'red alert' to merely feeling stressed. Similarly, if you're stressed, it can feel wonderful to slip back into cruise mode, or 'balance'.

You can shift from 'panic' to 'stress', or from 'stress' to 'balance' very quickly, if you know how. Since stress is painful, the body wants to get out of it. All it needs is some encouragement. It only take a few seconds of a 'spot-meditation' to do it. If, for example, you stop what you're doing, take stock, have a few deep breaths and sigh, you can take your body down a notch or two quite rapidly. The full instructions for this are at the end of this chapter.

Spot-meditations can be very brief, and if you do several a day you will disarm the stress response or at least keep it manageable. This is meditating in order to be relaxed during the day. The short meditations bring you back into daily balance, or 'cruise' mode. The long ones give you deep relaxation, but they usually need about 10 minutes or more. Both kinds are invaluable.

A CLEAR MIND IS NOT BLANK

Tension and relaxation are relatively easy to understand. They are part of a clear physical process whose symptoms are obvious once you know how to look for them. However, the other goal in meditation, clarity of mind, or awareness, is more subtle and much misunderstood.

Many people are discouraged from meditating because of a simple misconception: they assume the mind has to go blank. Or that they have to stop all thoughts or block them out. This is an impossibility. If you went completely blank, you would have no awareness of self or place. You wouldn't be there to know what that state is like.

So meditation, no matter how deep, is always a conscious state. It has to be, if you are going to direct it or be aware of it at all. So you always have a subtle sense of self and what is happening. Also, because we are living beings, there is always some activity in the brain. While meditating, you need to lightly monitor those passing thoughts and sensations. Some of them at least are important.

If you question people who say, "my mind was completely empty", they usually mean that they're still aware of thoughts and sensations, but are not responding to them. They know where they are and what is happening in consciousness, but they feel detached and distant from it all. They can have a magnificent sense of space, stillness, and peace, and yet the mind is 'empty' only in comparison to what went before.

CLARITY OF MIND AND AWARENESS

So a clear mind is not empty. It is one that thinks clearly. It sees what is going on with clarity and detachment. It is able to sit back and watch and not rush to conclusions. It is the observer mind.

To be 'aware' means to watch thoughts and sensations without reacting to them. This is peaceful because it's passive. You don't have to do anything at all. You don't have to block out bad thoughts or hang on to good ones. You just step back and let them all flow through consciousness. This is sometimes called 'the mirror-like' mind, just as a mirror reflects everything equally, without attachment or aversion.

In an Indian metaphor, the mind is described as being like two birds. One is active and busy: it eats the fruit. The other is passive and still: it just watches the first. The first bird get things done, but the second is wise. It sees the big picture precisely because it's not involved. Meditation particularly develops that detached, observer mind.

Awareness is a kind of meta-mind behind your ordinary mind, watching what you're doing. Performers and sports people typically use both minds. They can both perform and monitor their performance at the same time. They know what they're doing as they're doing it.

This clarity comes more easily when you relax. When you are tense or anxious or excited, you are running on high emotion. Even if you're enjoying this, it doesn't lead to clear thinking. It's all too fast and confused. The mind glues itself to thoughts.

When you relax, however, the emotional charge fades and you burn energy at a lower rate. Your thoughts may not change, but there's less fuel to feed the fires. At the edge of sleep, the emotion fades even more, and you can't see why you were fussed at all.

Quite simply, a relaxed mind moves more slowly than a busy one. It doesn't leap so rapidly from thought to thought. It can stay with each one long enough for you to actually register it. You know what you're thinking about, and can direct your thoughts at will.

AM I DOING IT RIGHT?

Even people who meditate regularly will wonder if they're doing it right, and it is true that they might be missing something. However, if you remember that you are seeking a calm body and a clear mind, it is not that difficult to check.

At the end of a sitting, you can ask, "Am I more relaxed and clear-minded than I was at the start?" Your body is likely to feel heavy, still and settled. The breathing is probably light and soft. There are many other signs of relaxation that I describe more fully in Chapter 6. You'll usually be able to say, "Yes, I definitely relaxed to some degree in the last few minutes. The meditation worked".

Similarly, you'll be able to read the change in your quality of mind. The mind is likely to feel slower, more deliberate and more present. It may feel a little sleepy, or it may feel still and spacious and in control. In any case, you'll know, "Yes, my mind is calmer and clearer than it was." The next chapter explains how to get these results.

Spot-meditation: Seven deep breaths

This meditation only takes a minute or so. You can do it anywhere, at any time. You can even do it with your eyes open, while standing in a queue or waiting at the traffic lights.

When tense, we hold our breath, and the out-breaths tend to be short. This gives us a certain energy charge, so we can respond quickly to danger if necessary. In contrast, we only let the breath go completely when we relax and it feels safe to do so.

By breathing deeply and deliberately sighing, we mimic the physiological effect of relaxation. It sends signals to the mind saying, 'It's okay to relax now.' This is probably the fastest way to induce the relaxation response.

So breathe deeply and sigh seven times, but don't force the sighs. Just breathe in deeply, and then let go as much as feels right each time. Then wait for the new breath to come when it wants to. After three or four breaths, you'll find your whole body letting go in sympathy.

INSTRUCTIONS

Breathe deeply, sigh and pause. Wait for the next breath.
Breathe deeply again, sigh and pause. Repeat seven times.
Each sigh is usually deeper and softer than the one before.
Rest in that stillness at the end of the breath.
Seven sighs is quite enough.
Now enjoy the natural breathing as long as you like.

Chapter three

How it works:
the Principles

In this chapter, I'll explain the principles behind meditation. They're not complicated, but it is worth understanding why and how they all works. This gives you great flexibility regarding time, place and method. Without this understanding, people tend to blindly follow a formula, hoping it'll work out and not knowing why it often fails.

THE PROBLEM OF TOO MUCH THINKING

Much as we love and need to think, we often overdo it. To relax consciously and have a clear mind, we need to take a holiday from thought. If you're stressed, you're almost certainly thinking too much. That stream of worries, fantasies, plans and inner dialogues stimulates the body and mind and exhausts us. The price can be high: agitation, confusion, depression and illness. If it goes on for too long, we age prematurely and die young. It's toxic in high doses.

Unfortunately, the more we think, the worse we think. To think well at all, we need an occasional rest from thinking. A tired mind can't follow a train of thought and tends to scatter. It gets lost in trivia and frequently blanks out for seconds or minutes at a time, often while in a meeting or while driving. Sometimes we're just 'not here' at all. This is the opposite of a 'clear' mind.

In fact, it is the emotions behind the thoughts that are really the problem. While thinking may seem a rational activity, it's often powered by quite gross emotions. Fear (or 'anxiety', to use a more polite term) may be driving your thoughts about work. Anger or irritation may underpin your thoughts about family. Desire may be driving your planning for the weekend.

Some variant of fear, anger and desire drives most of our thoughts, even the satisfying ones. These emotions are chronic, rather than acute. They may not flare to the surface very often. They just chug along under all our thoughts, all day long, making us agitated and restless and confusing our judgment.

Their effect doesn't remain in the head. They send a continual drip-feed of hormonal signals to the body saying, "This is no time to relax. We've got things to sort out first." In other words, they activate the 'stress response', or the sympathetic branch of the nervous system, whose function is to mobilize the body for action. This is the opposite of relaxation.

You may have little to do on a pleasant Sunday afternoon, but if you're thinking a lot, you'll get tired. Worry will literally burn more energy than gardening or moderate exercise. You may be 20% or 30% more tense than you need to be for the ordinary activities of the day. This is why anxious or depressed people often feel wiped-out, even if they're doing nothing.

Even sleep is no escape from thought. It doesn't stop just because you're unconscious of it. If you wake a sleeper and ask him what was happening, he'll say he was either dreaming or thinking. And he can tell you what he was thinking about.

Thinking agitates your body and mind even while you are asleep. Many people wake up tired, knowing they've been busy all night. Or they sleep shallowly, or wake frequently, or wake too early, because of their nocturnal thinking.

Too much thinking keeps you more tense than you need to be during the day and unable to rest well at night. You feel as if you're never relaxed. It also makes the mind tired and cluttered and confuses your judgment. Meditation, as a tool for relaxation and mental clarity, is the antidote to all of this.

BE PRESENT, BE SENSUAL

How can we take a holiday from thought? How do we stop thinking about a dozen things at once? We can't blank out our thoughts or finish them off. You've probably tried those options and they rarely work, if at all. The effort to block thoughts will just make you tense. And since every thought comes with a tag leading to the next thought, you'll never come to the end of them.

However, just as antelopes can live safely in the company of lions, so can we escape our thoughts at will, if we know how. The strategy is simple. We divert our attention away from thinking into another function of the mind. We shift from thinking mode to sensing mode. Sensing utilises quite different parts of the brain, and pushes thinking into the margins.

'Sensing' means paying close attention to sight, sound, smell, taste or touch. When we focus on any of these, our thoughts temporarily drop into the background. They rarely disappear completely but, because they're no longer on centre stage, you'll start to relax.

This is the secret formula: be sensual. Shepherd the mind into the sense world. Come into the present. Taste the coffee, enjoy the evening clouds, sense your own body as you walk or sit, become a connoisseur of the moment.

Most of us know this instinctively. We often choose to relax by doing sensual activities. When we feel stressed, we have a cup of tea or something to eat. In that moment when you truly taste the cake, you're not thinking about yesterday or tomorrow. We may listen to music, or do exercise, or walk in the park, or play with a cat. Those moments when we're really there - touching, tasting, listening - break the circuit of our usual stream of thoughts.

It's not the cat or the cup of tea that makes us relax. The enhanced sensory input does it. We've got only a certain amount of mental energy, and if it goes into sensing, there is less available for thinking. Thinking and sensing are functions that inhibit each other.

Right now, if you put this book down, and listen carefully to the sounds around you for a minute, you would relax to some degree. I can guarantee it. But why does it happen? You may hear traffic, birds, a distant conversation or radio, then nothing much, then a sound from next door. Before you realise it, you will find your face and shoulders softening, and your breathing slowing down. That's pretty good, for one minute's effort. So why does listening to traffic noise have such an effect on your body?

Sensing and thinking make different electrical signals. Thinking produces 'beta' brain waves, which are fast, erratic and of low amplitude. Sensing produces 'alpha' brain waves which are slower, rhythmic and of high amplitude. You can read this shift on an electroencephalograph after just 20 seconds of sustained sensing. There is nothing fanciful or imaginary about this. Something very real is happening in your biochemistry.

Sensing and thinking are opposing functions. They relate to the 'relaxation response' and the 'stress response', which are the two opposing branches of the nervous system. They are the yin and yang, the alpha and beta, of our waking mind. Sensing relaxes you, and thinking activates you. You can understand these opposites in other ways as well.

Thinking is active; sensing is passive. Thinking involves past and future; sensing is about the present. Thinking is complex; sensing is simple. Thinking burns energy; sensing conserves energy. Let's look at these in more detail, since they explain how meditation actually works.

SHIFTING FROM ACTIVE TO PASSIVE

Thinking is active. You're trying to sort something out or to process your feelings about the day. Or you're trying to plot your schedule, so you can get what you want and be happy. Not surprisingly, this all takes effort.

Sensing is more passive. To listen carefully to the sounds around, you have to sit back and wait for the next sound to come to you. To taste something, you have to let the flavour gradually spread through your mouth. To sense things well, you let them come into your space in their own time. Sensing is about being attentive and passively noticing what is happening. This is also called 'being aware' or 'being present'.

Sensing is like the listening or receptive phase of a good conversation. You're not talking or 'doing' anything, but it is still a skill. The mind has to be relatively quiet to absorb what is coming in. Sensing enables you to exactly notice the detail of a flavour, the subtlety of a colour, the location and quality of a sensation in the body.

Sensing is slower than thinking. Thinking is typically fast and jumpy: you might have a hundred thoughts and shifts of focus in a minute. When we are in sensing mode, on the other hand, the mind moves more slowly. It draws you more deeply into things. Whereas we tend to jump from thought to thought, we glide from sensation to sensation.

BEING IN THE PRESENT

Most of our thoughts are about the past and future. We spend very little time in the present - probably two or three minutes an hour on average. We live in our minds, and only check into the sense world for a second here and there, so we don't bump into doors or get killed crossing the road.

Most of our anxieties are about the past and future. Both are frustratingly uncertain and out of our control. We can spend hours with our hopes, fears, fantasies and interpretations and rarely feel satisfied. Although we can only experience life in the present, we can get hopelessly lost in our thoughts about our thoughts about the past and future.

We can escape this confusion by consciously entering the present. The world of the senses can be a lovely space, full of light and color and beauty that we miss if we are lost in inner dialogue. The world turns from black and white to colour. This is the paradise we escape to when we leave the past and future behind. It's right under our noses. We can't live here and never think of other things. But we can walk into it whenever we like.

Being more in the present has enormous advantages. We actually know what we feel and see and hear and taste, as it's happening. We notice our emotional responses and inner feelings in more detail. We feel more grounded and our thinking has a more solid base.

BEING SIMPLE, DOING ALMOST NOTHING

Paradoxically, meditation is difficult to understand because it is so simple. I've taught it to five-year-old kids and they get it without difficulty. Even teenagers do better than most adults.

Adults, however, live in a world of mental complexity. They find it hard to imagine how anything this simple could work. They tend to think, 'Yes, I understand how to meditate. Just be present, focus and let thoughts go.' They forget that understanding alone is not enough. Meditation, like any skill, needs to be practised to bear fruit. Or they think, "Is that all there is to it? I must have missed something."

As mature, intelligent adults, we are used to thinking in complex and elaborate ways. We often juggle multiple trains of thought at once, and are modestly proud of our ability to do so. We usually feel we have to 'do' something to achieve anything at all.

Meditation, however, is a skilful kind of non-doing. It takes us back to a more child-like and passive state. It is a state of 'being' rather than 'doing'. Ideally, you sit still and do nothing at all. The less you try to do, the better it works. The body and mind return to balance precisely because you are doing so little.

However, the mind is very reluctant to do nothing at all. Even a calm mind is naturally exploratory and curious. So in lieu of doing nothing (which is impossible), we do something as simple and undemanding as possible. You just listen to sounds, or feel the breath rise and fall, or say a word over and over. You move from the noise and confusion of the hundred mental activities to the simplicity of just one. Meditation is about doing a simple thing, but doing it well.

It is like distracting an upset child with a toy. Soon the toy become more attractive than the worries. The meditation object is not important in itself, but the resulting state of mind is. Focusing on something simple diverts the mind from the stimulating effect of 'serious' and 'important' thinking.

Meditation is radically simple: you just sit still and do as little as possible. This calms the body and lets the mind settle. This concept can be a little difficult to grasp at first. Of all the good lifestyle things we do for ourselves - exercise, good eating, recreation - this is the only one that emphasises non-doing rather than doing. Many people find it a real struggle to do nothing at all.

CONSERVING ENERGY

When we think, the mind is active, doing complicated and emotionally-charged things and moving through the past and future. This burns energy, actual kilojoules in the body. When you meditate, however, the mind is passive, is doing something simple and is in the present. This saves energy.

Stress is a state in which you burn a lot of energy. It is actually the fight-or-flight response. When we are physically or mentally active, we need lots of energy to meet the perceived challenge. We say that the metabolic rate, or the rate at which you burn energy, is high.

Conversely, relaxation is a state in which you burn very little energy. It is the reverse of the fight-or-flight response. When we are in deep sleep, we use very little energy at all. In this state the metabolic rate is low.

The metabolic rate naturally rises and falls during the day. Paradoxically, the body does the critical work of self-repair only when the rate is low, when you are relaxing or asleep. Similarly, the mind needs the low energy states of sleep and dream to process the emotional events of the day and so restore its balance.

Meditation is the art of consciously lowering the metabolic rate. It is like finding that dial in the mind that winds down your overheated brain. We're all good at turning that dial up. Worry, excitement, busyness and coffee do it immediately. But once we're up there, we don't know how to turn it down again.

This is where the spot-meditations come in. If you're feeling stressed at work, just a minute's meditation - listening to sounds, or counting the breaths - will take you out of the stress zone into a more balanced state. You've wound your metabolic rate down maybe 20%. For the minutes that follow, you will be burning 20% less energy than you would otherwise.

You can think of meditation as an energy conservation technique. If you do a few 'spot-meditations' each day, you will save a huge amount of energy in total. The stresses won't pile up, you'll pace yourself well, you'll enjoy the day more and you'll feel less tired by nightfall.

These short meditations are also very time-efficient. You get a lot of benefit per minute. Five short sessions during the day will be much more helpful than one long one at the end.

BOTH RELAXED AND ALERT

People often ask me, "What is the difference between meditation and relaxation?" They correctly suspect that meditation is more than just being half asleep.

Meditation balances relaxation and alertness. Usually we are one or the other - wired up but not relaxed, or relaxed but half-asleep. When we start a meditation, we emphasise the relaxing aspect to get out of the stress zone. But when we've succeeded in this, and we're at the edge of sleep, we have to sharpen the mind to maintain balance. With fine-tuning we can achieve the best of both worlds.

We usually think of relaxation as a state in which the mind wanders. It goes from thoughts to feelings to daydreams to sleepiness, and is usually rather vague and out of control. When you meditate, however, you stay focused. You keep your hands on the steering wheel. This makes the mind still and clear in a way that daydreaming won't.

You could say meditation is the art of staying awake as the body goes to sleep. We normally lose consciousness at the point of sleep. It is a beautiful place and it's tempting to abandon ourselves to it. A good meditator, however, will hover on the edge, protracting the pleasure enormously. This is where the bliss states in meditation occur. Though profoundly rewarding, they are also quite subtle and delicate, and you will miss them if your mind is foggy or wandering.

RESTORING BALANCE

Because the formula is so simple - 'be present, focus on one thing at a time and let thoughts go' - some people aspire to make their whole life a meditation. It really doesn't work this way. It is not that thinking is bad and relaxation is good. Too much relaxation can make you lethargic and depressed, and unable to focus on anything at all. It is the balance that matters.

Relaxation is only half the picture. We still have to be active and emotional and to think about the past and future. Thinking is very, very useful. We just need to balance it with the slower, deeper states of mind.

Thinking and sensing, tension and relaxation, are the yang and yin of our waking mind. They support each other beautifully. If you relax and sleep more deeply, you have more energy and you think better. So the secret of a good, busy life is to relax well.

'Be present, be sensual, be simple.' If you understand these principles, you can apply them in an infinity of ways. You don't have to sit still with your eyes closed in a dark room for twenty minutes to meditate! That's just square one, and not even the best square to start with, for many people.

This formula is yours to play with. If you are imaginative and intelligent about it, you won't be stuck with set rules about how to meditate. If you remember what you are trying to do - relax the body and calm the mind - you can check whether it's actually working or not.

It is common for how-to books, and for meditation teachers, to give out 'one-size-fits-all' instructions. I'll give you more choices here, but if you keep the principles in mind, you can develop a style that suits your personal idiosyncrasies. If you're imaginative, you'll usually enjoy your meditations all the more.

Meditations can blossom in the most unusual places - while swimming, or eating or making love. While sad, or sick, or panicky. On aeroplanes, in the toilet, or at the dentist's. You can shift into sensing mode, and so relax, in all these circumstances. Just keep the principles in mind and improvise with them.

Spot-meditation: Where am I ?

When you're caught in a train of thought, you can literally lose contact with reality. Have you ever been driving or walking somewhere, and realise you don't have a clue where you are? This exercise takes you back into the world of sight, sound, smell, taste and touch. Two or three minutes is usually enough.

INSTRUCTIONS

1.   Ask: "What am I seeing?"
     (What is in front of your eyes? Sense the room with your peripheral vision. What are the most obvious visual features?)

2.   Ask: "What am I hearing?"
     (Explore the soundscape. Check out the sounds from all directions.)

3.   Ask: "What am I touching?"
     (Notice the points of contact: feet, buttocks, back, forearms, fingers. Feel the air on your skin.)

4.   Ask: "What am I smelling or tasting?" (if appropriate).

5.   Slow down and go deeply into any sensory data.
     Move from one to another as you wish. Notice when you inadvertently slide back into thought. Notice how still and focused the mind feels when you return to sensing.

Chapter four

How to do it: the Instructions

USING A MEDITATION OBJECT

The principles of meditation are simple enough: be in the present, be sensual and just watch the passing thoughts with detachment. But understanding the principles is not enough. They need to be streamlined into workable instructions.

Nearly all meditation practices have similar instructions. To help you be in the present, they get you to focus on *one thing* in the present. We call this the Meditation Object. It's your anchor. It's what your mind revolves around. You keep returning to it when you get lost.

The difference between meditations is the object you focus on. If you focus on the breath, it's called a breath meditation. If you scan the body, it's a bodyscanning meditation. If you listen to sounds, it's a sound meditation. If you look at a candle, it's a fire meditation. If you say a word or phrase repeatedly, it's an affirmation or a mantra meditation. Although you could focus on almost anything, these few objects above are the basis of most meditations you will find anywhere.

So why do you have to focus at all? Why can't we just let go and relax? If only we could! We've probably all tried to and failed. We lie in bed and try to sleep, but our thoughts keep us awake. We need a strategy to stop succumbing to thoughts, and that strategy is to focus on something else.

It's largely a matter of speed. We commonly try to process dozens of thoughts, sensations and problems in a single minute, and it's all too fast. Focusing slows down and simplifies that profusion of thought. The meditation object acts as an anchor, creating a drag on the mind.

A slower mind is better able to assess what's important and what's not. The useless and unimportant thoughts drop away more quickly. We feel calmer, and start relaxing. This is one reason why anchoring the mind on a single object is the key strategy in meditation.

CORE INSTRUCTIONS

'Focus on one thing, and let everything else go'.

These are the underlying instructions for nearly all meditations. The 'everything else' is all the other thoughts, sensations, memories, images and feelings that stream through the mind. Ideally you 'just watch' them stream by without engaging them. Some thoughts, however, stick to you like glue. Some sweep you away like a stampeding herd. Others are gently seductive, and some just want to talk and talk and talk. . .

Collectively, we can call this 'the mind-stream'. Meditation doesn't get rid of the stream. It just allows you to step back from it. You can't stop thoughts arising, but it's your choice whether you pursue them or not. Since we can't avoid noticing them, we can refine the instructions: 'Focus on one thing, and watch other thoughts and sensations with detachment'.

You'll notice the instructions are in two parts, and involve two quite separate skills. Focusing is relatively easy to understand. 'Watching with detachment', or 'observing', or 'being passively aware' is more subtle. However, both skills - let's call them 'focusing' and 'awareness' - are essential. You need them both.

A TYPICAL MEDITATION

So what usually happens when you meditate? Let's assume you decide to focus on the breath. So you tune into it. You feel it rise and fall. You feel the body expanding and contracting. You're now more or less in touch with the breath.

However, the world is full of temptations. After a few seconds, the mind says "Okay, I've got that. What else shall I do while I'm meditating?" Without telling you, it sneaks off to something else. Soon you realise you're thinking about last night's TV, or your girlfriend or what you have to do tomorrow, and the breath is nowhere in sight. These thoughts are quite exciting, so the mind speeds up.

'Focus on the breath' seems a simple thing to ask, but we keep losing it. It is reassuring to know that it happens to everyone. I've been meditating for 30 years and I still lose it. It's not that a good meditator is never distracted. His skill comes in abandoning a distraction fast. He spends a second rather than a minute with it.

Thoughts tend to catch us unawares and drag us along. Much of our thinking is barely conscious. We often don't know why we are thinking about this or that. But once you notice that you're thinking, you have choice. You can process that thought the way you normally would, or you can drop it.

If you let it go, you are free. You are detaching from something that stirs you up, and returning to something simple. You might have to do this hundreds of times in a session. This is the spade work of meditating. You can't avoid noticing the thoughts, but you can learn to detach from them quickly.

Just the intention to let thoughts go is enough to start you relaxing. As you calm down, it becomes easier to stay focused. Then you notice something interesting. You're aware of thoughts and sensations calling your attention, but you can resist them easily. They no longer distract you from the breath. In other words, you're able to 'watch other thoughts and sensations with detachment.'

If you're at all tired, your fatigue now emerges and you can rapidly sink towards sleep. You've switched on the relaxation response by disarming thoughts, but now it's hard to focus at all. It is very tempting to let the mind wander and daydream when you feel relaxed. Pleasant as this is, the mind never really settles.

At this point, you are half-successful. You wanted a relaxed body and a calm mind, and at least you've got the first half. Many people are quite happy with this. It is a genuine achievement to relax to this point, but meditation offers you more.

If you want clarity of mind, you'll need to stay alert. When you're focused and you know it, the peripheral thoughts can't get a foothold. The mind becomes delightfully calm and clear and in control. Once you get a taste for this deep stillness, it's much easier to resist the temptation to drift.

FOCUSING: YOU CAN'T DO WITHOUT IT

Focusing and awareness are the two critical skills you use in meditation. They seem obvious, but in fact you get better and better at them as the years go by. Let me describe them in more detail.

Focusing is about directing your attention where you want it to go. It is the opposite of letting the mind ramble. It's a natural skill. You couldn't do the shopping or clean the house without paying some attention to what you're doing. We can't really achieve anything without it. Meditation just improves this skill.

The ability to focus is more important than the object you focus on. The breath, the body, sounds, a repeated word, are common objects, but you could also focus on an activity, such as swimming or yoga or dance or craft work. Or an image, such as a flower or the ocean. Or a mood, such as peace or relaxation. Or a concept, such as God or emptiness. All that matters is that you choose a meditation object, and return to it when you get distracted.

Some meditations seem to lack a point of focus. They just ask you to let go, or empty the mind, or be peaceful, or wait for God to speak to you. In these cases, the meditation object is implicit rather than obvious. You are still directing your attention to an objective, and letting other thoughts go by.

Because some people find it difficult to focus, they occasionally dismiss it as not necessary. "I can relax perfectly well without focusing", they say, but their manner usually betrays their restlessness.

FOCUSING CAN BE VERY SATISFYING

Focusing is like focusing a camera. It highlights the object in the foreground and puts other things in the background. It makes you slow down and pay attention. For example, it is quite possible to eat a peach mechanically, barely tasting it at all. If you pay attention, however, you feel your teeth breaking the skin, the juice on your tongue and saliva flowing. You notice the freshness, the mixture of taste and smell, and even hear the sounds of eating. Focusing magnifies your pleasure.

This is good focus: it catches fine detail, like focusing a camera. Whether we focus on a peach or on the breath, all the principles discussed in the last chapter come into play. We are in the present, passively sensing and doing something simple. The turbulence and complexity of thinking is pushed into the background.

Focusing is enjoyable. It occurs naturally when something attracts us - a cloudscape, a flowering bush, a beautiful body walking by. A child absorbed in a toy is focused, sensing and present. This is a kind of unconscious meditation. The Indian word for focusing - 'samadhi' - is a synonym for tranquility and bliss, not effort.

Yet many people do try to focus in a way that is bound to fail. With knitted brows and grim determination, they try to nail their mind to the object and block out the thoughts. This macho approach is occasionally described in the literature. It is based on a subtle hatred of our thoughts and sensations. Just occasionally this works, but at what price?

Focusing doesn't destroy thoughts. It just puts them in their place. Meditation shouldn't be seen as a secret war against thinking. It is tempting to demonise our thoughts when they overrun us, but they do have a right to be there. We just need to keep them in perspective.

We can't force the mind to focus, but we can gently encourage it. Eventually the mind wants to focus because the results are so satisfying. The mind feels clear, awake and in control, and the body becomes delightfully still. This doesn't happen if you just daydream or space out. And it certainly doesn't happen if you follow your thoughts.

AWARENESS :THE SECOND SKILL

Even in a meditation when you're well focused, you're still likely to notice a stream of thoughts and sensations in the background. One thing after another catches your attention. If you took an inventory, it might go something like this: car-horn, sore neck, thought about work, restlessness, thought about food, sadness, a memory of yesterday, a forgotten task, birdsong, heaviness, pleasure, a blank space, itchy nose, peacefulness, a bright idea, muscle release, an item for the to-do list, a dream image and so on.

This is the stream of consciousness. It is the natural activity of the mind. It never dries up. We have to live with it, just as we do with the sounds around us. It is how we respond to it that makes us tense or relaxed. Most of the thoughts and sensations we never notice. Some we notice but dismiss instantly. Others grip our attention for longer, and some we obsess about.

Paradoxically, being passively aware of the mindstream is more relaxing than trying to ignore it. Just noticing thoughts tends to prioritise them and put them in place. This has an organising effect. It tells you what your mental preoccupations are in this moment. You relax in part because you know where you're at.

The trick is to monitor the mindstream with a light touch. Instead of processing a thought for 25 seconds, you give it 2 seconds. That's quite enough to register what it is, how important it is, and whether it needs attending to immediately (usually not). You don't have to get into a dialogue with a thought. It is said, "You can't stop birds flying overhead, but you can stop them nesting in your hair."

Both the focusing and watching functions will relax you, but by different mechanisms. Focusing is a temporary escape from the thoughts, like taking a holiday. Awareness, however, is relaxing because it puts you in a 'witness' or 'spectator' role. As the spectator, you can watch the show without getting sucked into the drama.

FOCUSING AND AWARENESS WORK TOGETHER

These two functions, focusing and watching, alternate during a meditation, and can even seem to occur simultaneously. Focusing acts like a spotlight, illuminating the object. Watching is like a floodlight, picking up peripheral data.

The meditation object is your anchor. It's home base. You spend a lot more time there than anywhere else. It gives you the stability you need to be aware of thoughts without being seduced by them.

Meditators often make themselves miserable by thinking that focusing is 'good', and that noticing other thoughts and sensations is 'bad'. They often want to 'get rid of' their obsessive thoughts, or 'block them out', or 'put a bullet through them'. When they find that focusing on an object can often dispel thoughts to a miraculous degree, they then assume that with perfect focus, the thoughts would disappear. Unfortunately, that just won't happen.

You can't fix the mind on an object like putting a pound of butter on a table. Within a few seconds it will attend to the background as well. It goes on a quick border patrol to check what else is happening. The mind is like a wild animal that feeds while periodically lifting its head to look for danger.

This oscillation between foreground and background is inevitable and natural. The mind rarely stays focused for more than 10 seconds before it also notices something in the periphery. Whenever it's picking up a background sound or sensation or thought, it's no longer 100% with the meditation object. Nonetheless, it can still be very calm.

Just watching the mind-stream with a light touch doesn't break your relaxation. In fact, it helps. Being passively aware of your subliminal thoughts actually breaks their power over you in a way that ignoring them doesn't.

Although most meditators understand focusing, many don't grasp the art of awareness. Unless you can learn to tolerate the thoughts and sensations you don't like, your meditation will always be vulnerable. You can't push them aside forever.

Focusing is a temporary escape from thought, but can't be sustained indefinitely. It's like having a good time on holiday: you still have to come back and face your problems at home. They don't go away because you've temporarily forgotten them. Awareness, however, enables you to relax in the midst of the inner and outer turmoil. You don't have to escape. You just look at everything with tolerance and a certain philosophic humour. Anywhere, anytime, in any situation, you can reduce your stress by switching into watching mode.

Spot-meditation: Zoom Lens

This meditation aims at high quality focus for a short time. Less than a minute is all you need to break the momentum of thoughts. The exercise below uses a visual focus. You could equally well focus on a sound or a tactile sensation, if you prefer to close your eyes.

INSTRUCTIONS

1.   Take a deep breath or two, and let your body relax.

2.   Now focus on to anything in your field of vision: the letter 'T' on the title of a book, the edge of a leaf, the pattern on a plate. Increase the magnification. Go right into the detail and enjoy it.

3.   "Name' it silently as you breathe out: 'T' or 'leaf' or 'pattern.' Play with it in your imagination if you wish. What does it remind you of?

4.   Feel your body and mind relaxing into the activity.

Getting Started

SO MANY OPTIONS! WHERE TO START?

All meditations have similar instructions: focus on one thing and let everything else go. However, there are thousands of ways of applying these instructions. You have many options about the posture, the place, the length of time, and the kind of object or activity you chose to focus on.

Let's look at posture, for example. Sitting, walking, standing and lying down are all classical meditation postures. These can be extended into activities, such as swimming, yoga or craft work or into routine daily tasks like cooking, washing, eating or dressing. You can be focused and in the present in all of these. These are all traditional meditations in the East.

Similarly, the meditation object is optional. While this is usually sensory, you could also focus on an image, a memory, a feeling, a concept or even a philosophic question. More about these later.

Time and place can vary. You don't need a quiet place and 20 minutes to meditate. Some sittings might last one minute, and others three hours. You can meditate in silence, out in nature or in a temple, but you could also meditate amid the noise and bustle of a city street or a hospital.

Despite this huge range of options, most meditators throughout the world will start in a very similar way. They will sit in a quiet place with their eyes closed. And they will focus on the breath, or the body, or on the sounds around or on a repeated word or phrase. This is what really works for most people. It is a good place to begin. The next few chapters will cover this territory in detail.

POSTURE AND PLACE

Let's assume you're a complete beginner about to do your first sitting. First you choose your place and time. Most of us have access to a relatively quiet place. A bedroom, living room or backyard will do fine. As you will see, it doesn't have to be perfectly silent.

Then you choose your time. Early morning or the evening is often the best, but any time is productive. Give yourself 15 or 20 minutes when you're unlikely to be disturbed. Put your watch in front of you so you can glance at it during the session, if you wish.

Then choose your position. An upright padded chair is usually best. If you are anxious that you won't be able to relax at all, then go for comfort: use a reclining chair or lie on the bed.

If you have my set of three CDs, then play the first guided meditation. This is the most luxurious way you could learn to meditate. Otherwise, follow the instructions below.

THE BREATH, THE BODY AND SOUNDS

In any meditation you do, you'll still occasionally notice your body sensations, your breath and the sounds around you. They are a given in any meditation, and they blend together very naturally. Since you can't avoid them, you might as well be able to focus on them. In the exercise below, we meditate on all each in turn.

These three are also the starting point for other practices. They are the main branches of the tree from which everything else emerges. In Chapter 6, I will give you extra ways of focusing on the breath. Chapter 9 presents your options for meditating on the body. Chapter 11 extends the sound meditation. Chapter 22 will take the breath and body practices even further.

COPING WITH DISTRACTIONS

Chapter 13 is on 'Awareness', but you'll find the seeds of it here. In any meditation, you're bound to get distracted occasionally. When this happens, your first strategy is to re-focus on the breath. Some distractions, however, are difficult to break free of. This is when it helps to use a little technique called 'naming the distraction.'

So if something is really bugging you, you step back from it and ask, "what is this?", and label it. If you're thinking about work, you say 'work'. Or 'food' or 'Peter' or 'headache' or 'traffic noise'. You see it objectively, 'just as it is'. This is what we call 'awareness' or 'passively watching'.

Naming a distraction disentangles you from it. You have to stand outside it to label it. It may not go away, but it no longer dominates you. Once you've acknowledged it, it's usually easier to return to your object.

Some people use imagery to help. They imagine putting the distraction on a shelf. Or dumping it in a garbage bin. Or seeing the mind as a stream of consciousness, and throwing it back in the stream. These are all ways of noting a distraction dispassionately.

WHAT IS LIKELY TO HAPPEN WHEN YOU MEDITATE

A meditation typically goes something like this. The first two or three minutes are often scrappy. The unfinished business of the day clamours for your attention as soon as you sit down. Gradually, you sort out the little bits and pieces and they lose their grip on you.

As you enter the present, sounds often seem louder and you feel the body in more detail. Your limbs may feel heavy and you notice your little aches and pains and fatigue. The out-breath feels loose and soft. These are the physiological signs of relaxation and they're worth noticing.

If you're at all tired, you can soon drop into a pleasant, daydreamy state. If you can stay alert, however, it gets even better. The mind detaches from thoughts, one by one, and becomes delightfully clear and still. The body literally goes into the first stages of sleep and feels peaceful and serene. In time, the peace and clarity come so often you take them for granted.

Remember that meditation works because it is so simple. The less you try to do, the more you relax. It really is a passive, watching state. If you distract your mind from thinking, you automatically relax. All I'm asking you to do in the meditation below is: listen to sounds, check out your body, feel yourself breathing and name whatever bugs you. You can manage that, can't you?

Breath, Body and Sounds

This meditation is on sounds, the body and the breath. I suggest you spend 1-3 minutes on each of them. Then spend the rest of the time focusing on whatever works best for you. You can also expect to lose focus from time to time, so 'name the distractions' whenever you need to.

INSTRUCTIONS

1. PREPARATION
   Adjust your posture and let the body soften.
   Breathe deeply and sigh four times.
   Be passive, 'just watching', doing almost nothing.

2. SOUNDS
   Just listen. Let sounds go through you.
   Wait for the next sound.
   Look for the quiet background sounds.
   Enjoy the spaces between sounds.
   Return to sounds if you drift back into thought.

3. SCAN THE BODY
   Scan your body slowly from top to bottom,
   like shining a spotlight on each place.
   Feel your body in detail, 'just as it is'.
   Let the sensations come to the surface,
   whether they're pleasant or not.

4. THE BREATH
   Go into the breath. Feel it rise and fall.
   Feel the body expand and contract.
   Let the breath be loose. Don't try to control it.
   Enjoy the breathing. It massages you internally.

5.   NAME THE DISTRACTIONS

Let thoughts and sensations pass by in the background. If a thought seriously distracts you, then identify what it is. 'Name' it, or put it on a shelf, or throw it in a river.

6.   ENJOY WHAT YOU ARE DOING

Focus on whatever will hold your attention: sounds, body or breath. Feel your body become heavy and still.

Chapter six

The Breath

THE MOST IMPORTANT MEDITATIONS

Whatever you focus on, you'll still periodically notice your body, the sounds around you and your thoughts. They never drop off the screen for long. If you focus on the breath, for example, you'll still occasionally notice that your body feels stiff and tired, it's rather noisy outside and you're thinking about money or your husband.

Not surprisingly, these four things - the breath, the body, sounds and thoughts - are also the most common things to meditate on. There are scores of ways to meditate on the breath or the body. Meditating on random sounds is a simple practice but very useful. And we all need some way of tolerating or 'just watching' the stream of consciousness.

The breath, the body, sounds and thoughts are fundamental practices. They are the bedrock. If we include meditations that use mantra, affirmations and visual objects, we have a very comprehensive range. I imagine 90% of the world's millions of meditators are using some variant of the above. This book covers them all, and a few more besides.

In this chapter, I outline the instructions for *any* meditation practice by using the breath as a example. Furthermore, when I want to illustrate a point later in this book, I will often use 'the breath' to represent 'any meditation object.' The instructions for 'The Breath Meditation' below are actually a template for any other practice. Only sections 3-5 specifically relate to the breath.

WHY THE BREATH MEDITATION IS SO POPULAR

The breath is always with us. We can focus on it anywhere, at any time. It is usually a soothing thing to tune into. The gentle ebb and flow of the breath massages the body internally. It is soft, tactile and reassuring. Perhaps it evokes memories of our time in the womb, when we were enclosed by our mother's heartbeat and breathing.

The breath gives us feedback. It tells us exactly how tense or relaxed we are. When tense, the breath feels constricted and held in the chest. As we loosen up, the breath drops through the body. Eventually, it becomes delicate, soft and spacious. We also notice how our thoughts can stir up the breath. It is a perfect mirror to what is happening in our bodies and minds.

The more we relax, the more subtle and evasive the breathing becomes. This forces us to stay alert to keep in touch with it. We also get a taste of stillness and deep space in the gap between the breaths.

The breath mixes well with other practices. It is transparent. It can act as an anchor or basis for other meditations. While focusing on the breath, we can easily scan the body or say a mantra or watch thoughts or listen to sounds or do a visualisation as well. The breath also seems to stimulate memory and dream imagery more than other practices.

The breath meditation is simple to understand and easy to do, yet it's also a practice that matures over time and can last you the rest of your life. If you just did this one practice well, as many people do, you wouldn't need anything else.

Although I've been talking up the breath meditation, you shouldn't assume that it's an integral part of every practice. It's not, and it doesn't suit everyone. It's the most popular practice, but millions meditate on other things. It's the act of focusing, not the object itself, that matters in the long run.

The Breath

INSTRUCTIONS

1:   PREPARATION
Sit in an upright padded chair in a relatively quiet place.
Adjust your posture and let the body soften.
Close your eyes if you want to.
Breathe deeply and sigh four times.

2.   COME INTO THE PRESENT
Shift from thinking to sensing.
Shift into passive, watching mode.
Let thoughts and sensations come and go in the mind.

3.   FOCUS ON THE BREATH
Go to some place where you can feel the breathing easily.
It could be in the belly or chest or throat or nostrils.
When you breathe out, let your mind sink into that place.

4.   GO INTO THE DETAIL
Feel the breath rise and fall, the body expand and
contract. Ride on the ebb and flow of the breath.
Don't try to control it. Just let it do what it wants to do.
Enjoy the sensuality of breathing.
Try to catch the start and finish of each breath.

5.   COUNT THE BREATHS
Count the breaths silently, up to 4, or 8, or 10 repeatedly.
Say each count on the outbreath: 'One . . . . two . . . .etc'.
Keep the count going amidst whatever else is in
consciousness.

6.   NAME THE DISTRACTIONS
     Come back to the breath whenever you get lost.
     If a thought or sensation distracts you, then 'name' it:
     'headache' or 'work' or 'chainsaw' or 'Mary' etc.

7.   FEEL THE BODY RELAXING
     Your limbs may feel heavy or still or numb or light.
     You may notice tingling, warmth or pulsing on the skin.
     Your aches and pains and fatigue may become more
     obvious.
     The breathing usually becomes lighter and gentler.
     Enjoy these sensations.

8.   EMERGE SLOWLY
     Have your eyes open for the last few seconds.
     Let them rest lightly on something in front of you.
     Keep the breathing and the face soft.
     Stay passive and enjoy the way you feel.
     Ask, 'Am I more relaxed and calmer than when I started?'

REVIEWING THE MEDITATION

Now let me explain some of the above instructions in more detail. When we start a sitting, we're usually more tense than we need to be. It's surprising how much you can soften the body and the breathing with a quick scan and three or four sighs. This should be a preliminary to any meditation, however short. Give it 20 seconds at least.

You don't have to sit perfectly still to meditate. Don't freeze up. Relaxing means letting the body go. Good meditators often move slightly from time to time. The face and shoulders soften, the breath becomes looser and little postural adjustments occur. Watching these sensations takes you deeper into the body and accelerates the process.

COME INTO THE PRESENT

This means noticing the body sensations, sounds and sights we normally ignore when we are thinking. Sounds typically seem more vivid when you start. Don't worry if some noises irritate you or your body hurts. Because the sensing function is naturally passive, and you're not trying to 'do' anything, the mind slows down anyway. The present is a safe place to be.

FOCUS ON THE BREATH

Focusing means 'bringing the object into focus', like adjusting a camera lens. This enhances detail and time slows down. You try to notice the very moment the breath starts and stops. Focusing is easier if you can get interested in your object.

Don't try to control the breath or, if you are a natural controller, at least control it lightly. This is not the time to do formal breathing exercises. Just use the breath as a prop to hang the mind on. Let the breath go completely when you breathe out, and let the new in-breath come when it wants to.

Because the breath is 'transparent', you're bound to notice other thoughts and sensations as well. The mind naturally oscillates from the breath in the foreground to the thoughts in the background. Don't try to hold the breath in an iron grip and block out thoughts. Remember the instructions are in two parts: 'focus on one thing, and watch other thoughts and sensations with detachment.' It's okay to watch.

COUNT THE BREATHS

If the mind gets too relaxed and passive, it's prone to drift. There is usually some simple repetitive task at the core of any meditation to keep you on track. In this case you count the breaths, to four or eight or ten breaths repeatedly.

Usually you say the count on each out-breath: 'one. . . two . . . etc'. It might help to double-count, saying 'one' on both the in-breath and the out-breath. Or you could just say 'in... out...' as you breathe.

Counting is easy at first. Then the mind puts the count on automatic pilot and wanders off to play. Counting is a warning device. It you can't remember what the next number is, you know you've lost the plot. You also know exactly what to do next. You drop the thought that has distracted you and start counting again.

Counting alone is not enough. You still have to consciously feel the breaths or you'll get lost in thought anyway. Counting is just a way of pointing you at the breath.

People usually count four or eight or ten breaths at a time, and then return to one. Musicians often just 'feel' the number they're up to, like sensing beats in a bar. I once had a class containing five accountants. Counting was not their idea of fun. If you're really in touch with the breath and you know it, then counting is an unnecessary prop.

AM I DOING THIS RIGHT?

If you do the above exercise a few times, you will certainly relax to some degree. But you might also wonder, 'Am I doing it right?', or 'Am I missing something?' or 'Can I do it better?' These are good questions. If you want to get good at anything, you need ways of evaluating what you're doing. In chapter 8, I will help you answer those questions.

Chapter seven

'Just Watching'
the Distractions

THE STREAM OF CONSCIOUSNESS

Meditation seems simple enough. You're just trying to focus on one thing and let the other thoughts and sensations pass by in the background. Why is it so hard to stay on track? And why do thousands try to meditate and give up in disgust?

They get distracted, of course. The 'other thoughts and sensations' seem to be, and actually are, more important than the meditation object itself. It's not surprising they call our attention. Let's have a look at what they consist of.

Every minute, thousands of thoughts and sensations go through the mind, even if we don't notice most of them. This stream of data never stops. If it did, we'd be dead. Since we perceive each one successively, it's easy to imagine them as objects floating down a stream, one after the other. This is what we call 'the stream of consciousness'.

When you meditate, you're bound to notice things other than the meditation object. Some are sensory: a barking dog, a cough or your shoulder feeling sore. Some are thoughts: you find yourself wondering "What will I eat tonight?" or think of last night's TV. Some are moods or emotions: you're worried about your sick mother or delinquent son, or you're vaguely irritated by life itself. Some are memories or images. If we're trying to relax, we'll feel most of these as unwanted distractions. However, the mindstream is not all negative.

When we unwind, the stream of consciousness becomes more beautiful. We feel the body relaxing deeply and the mind lightening up. Pleasant memories and sensations, images and insights, also flow down the stream. These are definitely not distractions to be ignored. These are the very reasons why we meditate.

Yet meditation seems to trivialise it all by saying, 'Focus on one thing and let everything else pass by'. Does the breath really deserve more attention than everything else put together? Why on earth do we focus on it at all?

FOCUSING HELPS ANCHOR THE MIND

None of our thoughts and emotions are inherently bad. It's just that their sheer volume and emotionality overwhelm us. We can't relax if we're being swept downstream by our compulsive thinking.

This is where focusing comes in. We escape our thoughts by finding a vantage point outside the stream. By getting a good grip on the breath, we clamber out of the stream on to the shore. Anything we focus on puts other things behind us, just as going to a movie or partying with friends makes us half-forget our difficulties at work.

Although the breath is important as a safe haven, it's not all that interesting in itself. It calms us down and help us come back to balance, but we don't meditate for this purpose alone. We also want a clear, alert mind that can see things dispassionately.

Once you're calm, you can more clearly see the contents of the stream. You see yourself in more depth. It happens automatically. The stream tells you what you are doing and how you feel in that moment. You notice the cocktail of thoughts, feelings and sensations that give you the experience of 'you'. This has huge benefits in time.

Focusing is your basic strategy. You can't do without it. It gives you a point of perspective. Unfortunately, people commonly forget about the need to also 'watch with detachment'. When they get distracted, they simply try to re-focus, and 'get rid of the thoughts'. This is not a recipe for success. Your satisfaction depends more on being able to watch your on-going thoughts and feelings objectively.

WELCOME THE DISTRACTIONS

Each time something distracts you, you have a little challenge. You've lost focus, but this is where you can make the mind a little clearer. Can you see that distraction just as it is, without reacting to it? If you can, your mind is free. That's the ideal, anyway: a cool, dispassionate, objective mind.

We always notice background thoughts and sensations when we meditate, but most of them don't need to distract us. Many are sensual things anyway. The sounds of traffic or a slamming door, a headache or back pain, a sense of fatigue all keep us in the present moment.

A thought is a much bigger distraction, and it can trap us quite fast. It sucks us away from the breath and engages us in conversation. Once we realise we're either fighting it, or generally giving it more attention than it deserves, we make our escape. This is where the technique called 'naming the distraction' comes in.

Thoughts usually need to be acknowledged before they let you go. If you're distracted, just ask 'What is this? What am I thinking about?' and identify it. To do this, you have to stand back from it and see it from outside. It's still there, but there's now some distance between you.

You 'name' the content of the thought: 'Television . . . food . . . work . . . money . . . Sally . . .' Labelling a thought is quite different from getting into a conversation with it. It holds it at arm's length.

'Naming the distraction' serves to pigeon-hole it. The thoughts around 'work' or 'Sally' don't disappear, but you don't indulge them. They are still in the mind but not centre stage. You allow them a place in consciousness, but at the periphery.

You could use very general words when you name. You could just say 'distraction', or 'past' or 'future', for example. You could be more precise and name the content of the thought - 'money' - or the emotion behind it - 'worry'. You could even name sensory things that are disturbing you: 'garbage truck', 'itchy nose', 'sore feet'.

Many people use imagery to help. They imagine they are filing thoughts away or pigeon-holing them. Or arranging them in piles on their desk. Or tossing the useless ones in a bin. Or throwing a thought back into the stream of consciousness.

Naming often dispels a distraction rapidly, but that is not its sole purpose. In that split second, you're also registering what the thought is and how important it is. This is useful to know, whether the thought distracts you or not. Ticking off the thoughts and sensations as they pass has an organising function. It sorts them out and puts them in their place. In other words, noticing distractions is not a distraction in itself. Done well, it helps you relax.

WATCHING WITH PLEASURE

When you start to sit, you're usually at the mercy of the stream of consciousness. There are lots of distractions and you struggle to get clear of them. When you're relaxed, however, you're outside the stream, looking at it from a distance, and nothing much distracts you. This is when you can shift into 'pure awareness', or 'just watching' what happens in the moment.

The meditation object is your doorway into the present, but once you're there, you don't need to stand in the doorway. You can tune into anything at random in the sense world: sounds, sensations in the body, even the quieter background thoughts and feelings in the mind.

The present is more tranquil than the world of thought, but it still changes continuously. Neither sounds nor the sensations of our bodies remain the same for more than a second or two. We can't take it all in at once. The mind naturally scans, moving serially from one sensation to another. Or, to put it another way, one thing after another catches our attention: a birdcall, a twinge in the neck, the sight of wind in the trees, a heavy feeling, a distant conversation . . .

The breath may still be your anchor, but you're effectively watching the stream of consciousness. This can make your sitting much more interesting. 'Being in the present' means to consciously notice one subtle sensation or feeling after another.

Spot-meditation: Naming the distractions

The first way you do this meditation is very brief - just a couple of seconds long. It happens within any longer meditation. When you get distracted, just identify what's caught your attention and let it go. Then return to the breath until the next time. That's it!

Otherwise, follow the instructions below. This is good to do when the mind is full of clutter. You still try to focus on the breath as much as you can, but you also let yourself identify the distractions without feeling bad about it. It's like taking an inventory.

INSTRUCTIONS

1.   Relax the body and breathing as usual.
      Focus on the breath or any meditation object.

2.   When you get distracted, don't be annoyed.
      Just ask 'What is this?' or 'What am I thinking about?'
      Don't rush. Let the object become clear and 'name' it.

3.   It may be a sensory thing: 'pain . . . traffic . . . cold . . .'
      Or a thought: 'work . . . money . . . holiday . . .'
      Or a feeling: 'sleepy . . . restless . . . sad . . .'

4.   You could imagine putting it on a shelf or filing it away.
      Or throwing it in a stream or a garbage bag.
      Or simply putting in in the periphery of the mind.

5.   Let yourself notice the distractions, but don't analyse
      them. And keep coming back to the breath.

Chapter eight

Understanding what Relaxation is

People often say to me, "I'm meditating regularly, but I don't know if I'm doing it right." This is a question they should be able to answer. Meditation is a skill, like playing a musical instrument or a sport. If you evaluate what you're doing, you can iron out the mistakes, improve your abilities and enjoy it much more.

Few people ask the obvious questions:

"What am I trying to do?"

"Am I getting what I want?"

"Can I do this better?", or even,

"Am I relaxing at all?"

WHY PEOPLE CAN'T EVALUATE THEIR PRACTICE

I have to congratulate anyone who is prepared to sit quietly for a few minutes each day. This will probably do them some good, whatever is going on in their heads. Unfortunately, many meditators fumble around in a fog, not knowing what they're doing. Let's look at some reasons for this.

Firstly, relaxation usually leads to unconsciousness. It's the process that takes us towards sleep, so we progressively lose awareness as we relax. Our thoughts wander and we tend to 'space out' a little. If we can't stay alert, it's hard to know what's happening.

Secondly, meditation is a state of 'not-doing', which is why it's such a valuable antidote to our busy goal-oriented lives. It is largely a passive activity, but you can get too passive with it. Once you realise how lovely it is to do nothing, you can get stuck there. People often feel it's good to blank out mentally. They sit down at the feet of a guru (or a tradition or practice), and let their intelligence die.

Thirdly, meditation is invisible to others. People often meditate poorly because no one can see what they're doing. Anyone can see you hit a bad golf shot, but when you sit perfectly still on your cushion, are you going into advanced states of trance or just worrying about money? Golfers continually give each other tips on playing better, but meditators don't. They rarely discuss their practice or learn from each other.

Finally, meditation is hard to talk about because it's largely a non-verbal state anyway. It is a shift from words to sensation, feelings and images, and rational thought seems out of place. If you also see meditation as an esoteric or transcendental experience, you're even less likely to ask, "Is this working?"

ASKING THE OBVIOUS QUESTION: 'AM I RELAXING?'

Meditation is about relaxing the body and clearing the mind, and these are intimately linked. If the body isn't relaxed, the mind is bound to be restless. A tranquil body is the foundation for beautiful states of mind, and you can't go far without it.

So a useful and important question to ask is, "Am I relaxing?" In this chapter, we'll look at checking your degree of physical relaxation and clarity of mind. Relaxing is not a spiritual mystery. It's a biological process that you can observe easily if you know what to look for. To relax quickly and deliberately, it pays to understand this humble process that we usually take for granted.

RELAXATION IS BIOLOGICAL

Let us assume you feel tense and anxious after a terrible day at work. As soon as you start to meditate, you feel the body loosening. You have initiated 'the relaxation response'. Within seconds, every biological system within you is changing from arousal to relaxation.

Muscle tension will release. Blood pressure will drop and circulation improve. Breathing will soften and the digestive system will come back to life. Your aches and pains will become more obvious then gradually fade away. If you stay alert and don't space out when you relax, you can notice all this happening.

There are also less obvious changes occuring with hormonal levels, immune system function, metabolic activity and so on. I detail these more fully in my other book, '*Why Meditation is Good for your Health*'. For our purposes here, it is quite enough to notice the obvious changes.

Our bodies, (and the systems with them), continually oscillate between activity and rest. The nervous system has the role of maintaining balance, and it operates like a thermostat. The sympathetic branch of the nervous system winds us up and the parasympathetic branch winds us down, according to the situation we find ourselves in.

In the 'up' or 'arousal' phase, initiated by the sympathetic system, we feel anxious or excited. Adrenalin and other hormones get to work. Muscles tighten, blood pressure and breathing rates rise, and we burn a lot of energy fast. This often feels good if it doesn't last too long. We can call this the 'stress' response. In extreme forms, it becomes the 'fight-or-flight' response.

In the 'down' phase, the parasympathetic system reverses all of this. Adrenalin levels fade, muscles relax, blood pressure and breathing rates drop, and we burn less energy as our metabolic rate falls. This is called the 'relaxation response'.

INITIATING THE RELAXATION RESPONSE DELIBERATELY

Everybody relaxes. We all fall asleep eventually. But we often don't relax well or deeply or long enough, and we're often unnecessarily tense during the day. We think the process should happen naturally when we want it to, but it often doesn't. We can wait for hours, trying to let go, and still feel tense.

By meditating, you can consciously turn on the relaxation

response when you want to. If you disconnect from the thinking process, the body can start relaxing within seconds. If you know how to steer it, you can wind the body down to the point of sleep within five minutes, changing all the body chemistry on the way.

This is a very useful skill, but it still works best if you know what you are doing. In other words, you need to stay alert as the body descends towards sleep. It helps to keep your hands on the steering wheel, rather than just letting go and hoping.

Meditation is very flexible. You could focus on the breath or a leaf or music or an image or a concept. Nonetheless, from time to time you'll still be aware of the sensations of your body. They're always there in the background, and you can use them to check what is happening. At any moment, they can tell you where you are on that sliding scale between complete tension and complete relaxation. They will also tell you when the process has got stuck part way.

Many changes occur, but the four main signs of relaxation I ask my students to look for are: heaviness, tingling on the skin, aches and pains becoming obvious and the breathing becoming lighter.

People who are sensitive to their bodies may notice them immediately. People who are reluctant to look at their bodies may not notice them much at all. But if you do notice them, they reassure you that you are relaxing well. If you actually focus on them, they act as a biofeedback mechanism and rapidly take you deeper.

HEAVINESS OR LIGHTNESS

"My body felt like lead."

"I felt I was sinking deeper and deeper into the chair."

"My hands felt numb, as if they were fused together."

"I couldn't feel my arms (legs, body). I wiggled my fingers to make sure they were still there."

Adrenalin provides a restless, chemical charge to the muscles. It makes them tense up, priming them for action. That charge fades when we start to relax. The muscles start to soften and stretch, and we lose muscle tone. For example the face may sag, and when the neck muscles let go, the head may bob forward.

Muscles make up 40% of our body weight. They're everywhere within us, and they're all losing tone as we relax. The mind interprets this sensation as a heaviness, especially in the limbs. We seem to sink into the chair. When you notice this, you know you've triggered the relaxation response.

Adrenalin also makes us restless, so we rarely sit perfectly still for more than a few seconds. Our subtle body movements activate nerve spindles in the muscles which send signals to the brain saying, "the elbow has moved one inch to the left" and so on.

As our body settles, those signals aren't triggered as much. The brain interprets this as the body feeling numb or light. At the edge of sleep, we may feel quite detached from the body, as if it's barely there at all.

If we stay conscious as we slip down towards sleep, we notice that the body tends to relax in the following sequence, with some stages overlapping: heavy, numb, still, light, disconnected, vanishing. The easiest to notice is the sense of heaviness. This comes from the feeling of tense muscles slowly stretching. If you actually focus on it, it will anchor you and take you deeper.

TINGLING OR WARMTH ON THE SKIN

"My skin felt warm and tingly."

"My hands and feet became quite hot."

"I felt warm in the meditation. I'm cooler now."

"I could feel the pulse in my hands (neck, face. . .)"

When we are tense, the blood flow is diverted from the skin to the large fight-or-flight muscles within the body. If you are terrified, your 'blood runs cold'. This is what you feel when the blood has drained from the skin. Have you ever wondered in ghost stories why an icy chill announces the presence of a spook? Now you know.

The reverse happens when we relax. The blood flows back to the extremities. The skin gets warm and tingly. It feels more alive, the same way it does after a shower or aerobic exercise or a shot of alcohol.

Usually the sensation is subtle, but for some people it is very obvious. Their hands may also get puffy and wedding rings feel tight. People who suffer cold hands and feet are often pleasantly surprised by the flow of warmth. As one woman said, "the room temperature feels just perfect."

The improved blood circulation also loosens up congested muscles, which become more soft and pliable. People sometimes describe this as a 'good energy flow' through the body. The stiff places start to soften. Many people will pick up the pulsing of the blood throughout their whole body.

ACHES AND PAINS SURFACING

"I didn't realise how tired and tense I was."

"I thought I was fine when I started to meditate. Then I noticed this awful headache and my stomach is sore too."

"It took a long time for the pain in the shoulders to go."

When we are tense we produce endorphins, which are the body's natural opiates. They numb the body out. We often feel fine when we're on overdrive because we're not feeling anything at all. This is the secret of a runner's high: the stress of running produces our natural opiates.

When we relax, however, the painkillers fade away and we gradually notice what we've been doing to our bodies. The little aches and pains all come to the surface - sore neck, headache, itchy skin or just that total body ache of fatigue. The long distance runner usually feels pretty awful when he relaxes after the race.

When you relax, you often feel a mild aching in the muscles. For example if you sit down after a couple of hours work in the garden, you'll feel quite good while the energy is still running through you. Five minutes later, however, you realise you're aching all over.

This is partly because tight muscles constrict the flow of blood. They get somewhat deprived of oxygen. When muscles relax and stretch, they allow more blood and sensation in. It seems that the aching feeling of fatigue is the result of mild oxygen deprivation.

This can upset people who want relaxation to be a totally pleasant sensation or a kind of oblivion. Because it often isn't, such people prefer to leap straight from tension into unconsciousness. Unfortunately, this is the push-yourself-and-collapse cycle. It's not a healthy way to live.

It's much better to relax into, and welcome, the aches and pains. This is a way of making peace with yourself just as you are. Their presence is a good sign that you are relaxing. Give yourself a pat on the back.

If you fight pain, you rarely relax well. Your resistance alone is keeping you tense. If you accept the natural discomforts of relaxation however, they usually sort themselves out fairly quickly. Pain that is part of the relaxing process can in fact be quite pleasant. It is like the 'good' pain you feel in a massage, when the masseur's fingers are loosening the sore spots.

A common sequence is 'no pain, more pain, less pain', particularly if you're meditating after a stressful day. First you feel no pain because the stress hormones are making the body numb and you're living in your head anyway. As you relax, the discomforts surface and you feel how the day has ravaged your body. By the end of the sitting, however, the headache is fading and the shoulders feel better. And by triggering the relaxation response, the loosening process continues after the meditation is over.

CHANGES IN THE BREATHING

"My breathing became quite light, and occasionally stopped."

"My breathing was quite erratic. Sometimes I had to sigh or take a deep breath."

"I felt I wasn't breathing enough."

"My breathing felt deep and lovely."

The way we breathe mirrors our levels of tension and relaxation. When tense, we tend to breathe from the upper chest only, and to hold the breath. This gives us a certain charge so we can respond quickly, if we have to.

As we relax, we gradually let the breath go. When people start to meditate in class I hear little sighs around the room. The shift from tense, upper-body breathing to loose, open breathing usually occurs in jerky stages over two or three minutes.

Eventually, the breathing can become very light and delicate. We breathe, after all, for a reason. We need oxygen to burn energy in the cells to maintain our level of metabolic activity. Tight muscles burn a lot of energy, even if they're doing nothing. When they relax, they need less energy, so we breathe less. The breathing now feels soft and spacious.

If the mind, which also burns energy, becomes very still, there can be a long pause between out-breath and in-breath. This can be a lovely moment, when the breath dissolves into space and everything seems to stop. This is when you know that peace is not just an idea. It's a physical experience, even if it only seems to last a few seconds.

OTHER SIGNS OF RELAXATION

Most people can notice the above signs of relaxation - heaviness, tingling on the skin, aches and pains, and changes in breathing. However there are also other indicators that are less common, and more specific to individual people. It is best to find out what your own landmarks are, so you know when you're on track.

For example, many people feel their stomach gurgling. Others have more saliva in the mouth. "I know I'm relaxing when I have to swallow", said one student. After a very stressful day, some people even feel a little nauseous.

These are all signs that the digestive system has started working again. In the fight-or-flight response, energy is diverted away from digestion to the big internal muscles, so we can run away or beat someone up. The digestive system closes up shop until we relax again. That's when the stomach starts to gurgle.

There are also many mental indicators of relaxation. These include a sense of peace or stillness or release or emotional flow. At the edge of sleep, some people see colours or fleeting dream images or old memories flash by. The mind may seem blank or at the edge of a beautiful darkness, or in a timeless state. You may feel very present, in your body and alert. Commonly, a person feels a serene detachment. She hardly feels her body and the issues that seemed so important now seem irrelevant.

RELAXATION IS A PROCESS

Strange to say, when we are tense nothing much is happening in the body. The mind is going wild but the body is locked up. Conversely, when we relax, the mind become still but big changes occur in the body. We don't instantly switch from being tense to relaxed. It's a fluid and dynamic process that usually takes eight to twelve minutes to complete.

We can say the body goes through three stages in most meditations - tense, relaxing and relaxed - and they are quite different in quality. Most of an average meditation is likely to be in the 'relaxing' phase. This means you're watching things that are constantly changing.

For example, the breath may typically go through the following sequence. It starts short and tight, then loosens with a sigh or two. Then settles down rather erratically, until it feels deeper and more rhythmic. Then typically it gets lighter and slower and occasionally stops. If you start thinking again, however, the sequence can even reverse and go back to an earlier stage.

HOW TO CHECK YOUR MEDITATION

First you ask yourself, "Am I relaxing?" and you look for the signs. Does the body feel heavy? Does the skin feel warm or tingly? Are you more in touch with the body as it is, including the aches and pains? Does the breathing feel soft? If you can answer 'yes' to any of these you know you're on track.

Then you could ask, "Could I relax some more?" And often you can. You may just need to let go that conversation in the back of your mind, or more consciously be in the present. You may find the body responds immediately. You drop that thought about work and something softens in your shoulders.

By meditating you're trying to relax the body and get the mind clearer. At the end you could ask, "Has it worked? Am I more relaxed and less caught up in thoughts than I was twenty minutes ago?" It's quite enough to be moving in the right direction, even if the steps seem small.

Don't hanker after for perfection. You might notice that a relaxed body is not automatically pain-free or filled with bliss. It's just relaxed. Nor is a clear mind automatically happy. It's just seeing what's going on with clarity. Meditation is not a 'happy' pill. If you're going through a divorce or an illness, meditation can keep you physically relaxed and mentally clear, which will help a lot. But don't expect to be perfectly happy about it all.

You can feel disappointed with your meditation for the wrong reasons. Often you're relaxed and clearer, but you still don't like the way you feel. You wanted that beautiful radiant feeling you got three weeks ago. Or you wish you didn't feel so exhausted. Even worse, you want the experiences that your teacher or your fellow students seem to talk about.

Aiming for an ideal state is setting yourself up for failure. It's far more sensible to remember your goal: relaxing the body and clearing the mind to whatever degree is possible. Meditation is a skill, just like playing a guitar, and you improve at any skill in small incremental stages.

SPOT-MEDITATIONS

It takes less than a minute to take the edge off your tension. If you give the body half a chance it will sink back towards balance in a flash. It takes five or ten minutes to reach total rest, but stripping away the excess tension takes almost no time at all.

We are all very good at tensing up. A coffee at breakfast starts the process. Driving to work winds us up a bit more. Then a demanding meeting or an aggravating encounter can rapidly lift our tension levels to the maximum.

But when the meeting is past, what do we do? We stay stirred up. We're not very good at winding back to a more balanced state. The spot-meditations help you find the 'you can relax now' button.

You can do them almost anywhere: sitting at your desk, walking down a corridor, at the toilet, standing in the lift. If you drop your metabolic rate just 20%, that means you burn 20% less energy for the next half hour or so. If you do several spot-meditations a day, you can keep yourself in balance all day long and hardly ever shoot up into the danger zone. You won't feel wiped out at 5.00 pm, because you haven't burnt out your energy reserves.

Spot-meditations take you back to basic principles: shift from thinking to sensing, be present, just watch, focus on something sensual. A spot-meditation is often just a very short version of a formal meditation. Once you understand the principles, you can apply them anywhere.

Spot-meditation: Red light

I took many radio interviews when the original edition of this book came out in 1993. The interviewers were fascinated by the idea that you could meditate in the forty-five seconds you were stuck at a red light. In fact, a television team invited me to fly across the continent to Melbourne so I could demonstrate.

A team of eight with a back-up truck met me at the airport. The car had a camera mounted on the bonnet, pointing to the driver's seat. It was a grey winter's day, so there were bright lights within the car itself, shining up on my face. So I drove off into rush hour traffic, late on a dismal Friday afternoon, to demonstrate the red light meditation.

This exercise works best if you are running late and the traffic lights turn red as you approach.

INSTRUCTIONS

1. You have been given a whole minute to stop and do nothing. Relax. Shake yourself loose and settle back in the seat. Take three or four deep breaths and sigh.

2. Scan your body for tension. How are you holding the steering wheel? Are your face and neck muscles tighter than necessary? Let your belly soften.

3. Be present. Look around you slowly. Notice the scenery, the traffic, the sky. Keep breathing.

4. This exercise finishes as the lights turn green. Now devote all your attention to the task at hand: driving safely. And look forward to the next red light.

Chapter nine

Scanning the Body

There are hundreds of practices based on the body and the play of sensations within it. For example, you can simply relax the muscles systematically from top to bottom. In yoga, you also focus on subtle energy flows and blocks within the body. In Tai Chi and Chi Kung, you focus on moving the body in a fluid, harmonious way.

The body is extremely useful to meditate on because the sensations change markedly as we relax. For example, when we're tense, we feel the body as being made of solid matter. This seems obvious, but as we relax, we experience the body more as a fluid play of sensations that come and go in consciousness. At the edge of sleep, we sense the body in an almost dreamlike fashion as being numb, or spacious and almost empty.

In this practice, we scan the body in deliberate stages, from top to bottom or bottom to top. We use the changing sensations in each place - tingling, pressure, pain or whatever - to hold our attention. This tends to bring the more subtle tensions to the surface, which alleviates many of them within seconds. It is like combing the knots out of a tangle of long hair.

BODYSCANNING AND THE BREATH

Obviously, this practice resembles the breath meditation. When you scan, you focus on the body while having a background awareness of the breath. In the breath meditation, you do the reverse. Nonetheless, these two practices appeal to different kinds of people. I call those who prefer the breath, 'still-mind meditators' and those who prefer to scan, 'moving-mind meditators.'

The breath meditation is usually more tranquil in effect. The mind ideally stays in one place and always returns to that place. There is a peripheral but not very detailed awareness of the body. This suits people who prefer simplicity and stillness.

Focusing on the gentle ebb and flow of the breath can be rhythmic and soothing. You can almost forget the body and go into slightly hypnotic states. In other words, you can be tranquil but not very alert.

The 'moving-mind meditators', however, find this approach boring and get easily distracted. They resent always returning to square one. They focus better if they have more to do. Since bodyscanning is more active, it suits people with active minds. With more to see and feel, it keeps them occupied.

Bodyscanning tends to make you very aware of your body just as it is, for better or worse. You also notice your thoughts and feelings more vividly. In other words, bodyscanning may be less tranquil than the breath meditation, but it enhances self-awareness.

When you focus on the breath, the body relaxes because the mind relaxes. It's as if you've found the master switch. Nonetheless, many of the minor tensions may still remain. Scanning the body, in contrast, is a more thorough way of releasing tension. You seem to find all the minor switches as well.

The detailed awareness does the trick. When you notice tension, say, in the shoulders, it invariably starts to release. If you don't notice it, it stays. This awareness also works for the hundreds of minor tensions in the body. When you scan, you seem to unlock each of those in turn.

THE EFFECT OF SCANNING

Whatever practice you do, it is always good to have a background awareness of the body. If the body is also your meditation object, you get a double-whammy effect. When you are focused, you can feel the physical consequences immediately. The mind and body form a biofeedback loop that can accelerate the process.

When you start relaxing, the breathing loosens and the pressures of the day drop from your face. The muscles soften and the limbs feel heavy. The deeper tensions and chronic rigidities come to the surface and loosen their grip. Eventually, you understand how each individual part of the body feels as it relaxes.

You also come to recognise the subtler effects of the relaxation response: soft breathing, more life in the digestive system, and a gradual sense of warmth and flow throughout. The 'energy-field' (i.e. the network of sensations in the body) becomes more fluid and alive. It seems as if you're nourishing all the cells of your body by just paying attention to them.

A meditator can illuminate the whole body from within. It is possible to see it in extraordinary detail, if you try, right down to the bones and organs. Many of us were taught to spend a whole hour doing one scan of the body from top to toe, or vice versa. This can be quite fascinating. The body is alive with sensation: tingling, pulsing, pressure, pain, bliss, the ebb and flow of the breath. It continually changes according to the activity of the mind and the depth of meditation.

Body-scanning often results in a profound sense of pleasure. It still surprises me that physical bliss can co-exist with the inevitable discomforts of having a human body. Some of my students even say that severe pain or illness are no obstacles. They can even help.

While most meditators have a reasonable degree of body awareness, some make it their speciality. Body scanning can have such extraordinary effects that I regard it as the most powerful of all healing meditations.

Yet because scanning is so therapeutic, people often try too hard to relax each place and make it feel good. This rarely works and can lead to frustration. Meditation relaxes us because it is a kind of 'not-doing' that is free of the effort that makes us tense.

The best quality of focus is a loving and tolerant curiosity towards the body, just as it is. This is what gives it permission to return to balance. You let your body talk to you and tell you how it feels. It likes to be listened to. All we can do is pay attention to it and gently explore without expectations. If you can feel at home in your less-than-perfect body, you automatically relax.

BODYSCANNING IS NOT ALWAYS PLEASANT

Bodyscanning can be unpleasant for some people because it tends to magnify sensations. It is a sign of good focus that you see your object in more detail than usual. Unfortunately, many of us are in pain, or are unconsciously afraid of, or resentful towards, our bodies. After all, our bodies don't always do what we want them to do, or feel the way we would like them to feel. They are largely out of our control.

By scanning we may also notice the emotions which accompany our tension. Our tight neck muscles or lower back pain may bring up feelings of frustration or despair. Chest pain or general discomfort may be interlaced with anger or resentment. Bodyscanning may highlight your dissatisfaction with yourself.

If, however, you see how your hostility makes your tension worse, you can do something about it. It's not easy to admit that your chronic back problem is unlikely to go away. But if you do, you relax more and the pain may be easier to tolerate. Both physical and emotional pain tend to release if you stop fighting them.

The formula is simple: accept yourself the way you are and most of your tension will go. Unfortunately, there are thousands of things we don't like about ourselves - sensations, thoughts, moods, habits etc. In meditation, we meet them one by one, as the seconds and minutes go by. Each one gives us the chance to let go a little more of our habitual negativities and so make peace with ourselves. The minor physical discomforts are a good place to start.

The results can be truly amazing. Though bodyscanning can illuminate our discomforts, it's also the royal road to bliss. You can feel every part of your body, and all the systems within it, returning to a state of health and balance.

Beneath the mild discomforts, the body can feel tranquil, radiant and vital. Because focusing magnifies what you focus on, you realise how good it feels just to be alive and conscious. It's all we need for deep happiness, and it gives the lie to all our efforts to find pleasure outwardly. This is why meditators are often so content for no apparent reason.

SCANNING OVER SEVEN STAGES

In the practice on the next page, we scan the body in 7 stages. If you want, you can spend 4 or 8 or 10 breaths in each place, depending on the pace you prefer.

This template gives you something systematic to do. It is useful to have a clear structure. If you plan to spend 10 breaths in each of those 7 areas, you know exactly what you are doing for the next 70 breaths. If the mind gets distracted, you pick up where you left off. If you last remember counting the third breath in the throat, that's where you get back on the train.

Neither scanning in stages nor counting the breaths are essential. They just give you a template. You don't even need to scan right through. If you feel that a tight shoulder, or a headache, wants lots of attention, then stay there. All that matters is that you're focused on your body and disengaging from thoughts.

Bodyscan

INSTRUCTIONS

First sit comfortably and shake your body loose, releasing any obvious tension. Take a couple of deep breaths and let go completely as you breathe out.

Scan the body at your own speed, noticing the subtle detail. You can count the breaths if you wish, spending perhaps four, or eight or ten breaths in each region.

1. Scalp and forehead
    (Notice tingling, pulsing, pressure . . .)
2. The face and lower part of the head
    (Soften the eyes. Let the mouth and jaw go slack)
3. Neck, throat, shoulders, arms and hands
    (Like stroking or massaging the body with your mind)
4. Chest and upper back
    (Feel the lungs expand and contract)
5. Diaphragm and solar plexus
    (Feel the movement of the lower ribs)
6. The belly and lower back
    (Feel the soft organs move slightly as you breathe)
7. Hips, legs and feet
    (Feel or imagine the breath dropping through your body)

Now let your mind rest wherever it wants to in the body. Watch the breath or heartbeat or any other sensation in that place. Stay there as long as you like or scan again, either up or down. Enjoy the feeling of the body relaxing.

Spot-meditation: Countdown

This is similar to the above but done more rapidly. It may take only a minute or less. Standing or sitting, eyes open or closed, in public or private, you scan the body over seven breaths. It's called the 'Countdown' meditation, because you can count from seven to one as you do it.

INSTRUCTIONS

1.   Breathe through the body over seven slow breaths.
     Each time you breathe out, you move down one region.
     Count as you do this: "Seven . . . six . . . five . . . four . .
     . .three . . . two . . . one . . . "

2.   Repeat as you wish. Or anchor the mind on any sight or
     sensation for as long as you like.

Chapter ten

Posture and Breathing

Our posture - the way we hold ourselves during the day - influences our state of mind more than we realise. The reverse is also true. If we are miserable or angry or frustrated, this is reflected in the structure of our bodies. Because our bodies and minds are two sides of the same coin, we can influence one by changing the other.

The yogic tradition places great emphasis on posture as the foundation for beautiful states of mind. In one Zen tradition, you were expected to spend a year just learning how to sit well before further instruction was given. These ideals are beyond most of us, since we're not aiming to become professional meditators. However, changing posture is the simplest way to relax quickly and improve the quality of your meditation.

WHAT IS GOOD POSTURE?

Posture is important, but it is much misunderstood. For example, many people never attempt to meditate because they assume they have to sit cross-legged on the floor. In fact you can meditate in any posture. The four classical Buddhist postures are: sitting, walking, lying down and standing. Since the aim was to be relaxed and aware all day long, you couldn't just do the practice sitting.

Nonetheless, in any posture, you should be comfortable (but not super-comfortable), balanced and open (so your breathing isn't constricted), and alert. You can't expect to meditate well slouched in an easy chair or curled up in bed. The general rule is: don't slump. If you sit against a wall, it's best to have a small cushion in the small of the back.

SITTING IN A CHAIR

In 1995, I was at a conference in California with 150 meditation teachers. I imagine every one of us had learnt to meditate sitting on the floor. However, at the conference about half of them were now meditating in chairs. Some had ruined their knees, pushing through the pain barrier all those years ago in Asia. But, for most of them, using a chair just worked better.

Most Westerners find a straight-backed, padded office chair is ideal. It should be low enough to have both feet firmly on the ground. If you are short, put cushions under your feet. Even better, cut the legs of the chair to the right size. Most chairs are designed for the average man and are too high for many women. I had two inches cut off the legs of half the chairs at my meditation centre.

Some people like armrests, and some don't. These can prevent the shoulders slumping and prop you up. They are good for the elderly and infirm or for you, at any age, if you happen to be feeling that way.

When sitting in a chair, the right-angle between torso and thighs can block the breathing a little. You can overcome this by spreading your legs apart and letting the belly hang out. This creates a tripod effect with your two legs and your bottom. This 'samurai' pose doesn't look very feminine but it supports your lower back well.

SITTING ON THE FLOOR

This is an excellent position if you are relatively supple and fit. Otherwise, it takes strain to hold and you soon tend to slump. The lower back balloons out and the shoulders collapse. This blocks the breathing and compresses the inner organs. If you're past thirty and not very flexible, it's usually not worth trying to sit this way.

Because muscles loosen up as we relax, we have a strong tendency to slump when we meditate. This is unhealthy for both the body and the mind. Slumped shoulders induce a slight feeling of depression, a kind of 'leave me alone' mood. If you let your shoulders slump right now, you'll notice what I mean. People who habitually meditate on the floor easily fall into this trap. The posture alone can induce a mild, masochistic gloom.

To sit well on the floor, you need *big* cushions, to get the hips well above the knees. Zen practitioners use solidly padded cushions that can be eight inches deep. These are large enough to tilt forward slightly when you sit on their edge. Personally, I like to put a smaller cushion under the back of the big cushion to increase the tilt. This throws the hips forward, supports the lower back well and opens the front of the body so you breathe easily. It is like sitting on an ergonomic chair.

Sitting without a back rest gives you a sense of independence and self-reliance. It also allows the body to move spontaneously and to adjust itself internally. The 'energy' moves up and down the spine more freely than if you're leaning against a chair, which is important in advanced stages of practice.

RECLINING CHAIRS AND LYING DOWN

A reclining chair or lying on the bed is ideal if you want to go to sleep. It's also good if you're elderly, or suffer neck and back problems, or if you're too sick or tired to hold an upright position without strain. People who suffer chronic anxiety, which is a state of hyper-alertness anyway, are also likely to meditate better in a reclining chair.

To use a reclining chair or to lie down usually means you're willing to risk going to sleep. It can be hard to stay alert when your body is totally supported. Nonetheless, these postures are good if you're just too tired to meditate otherwise. Given the kinds of lives we lead, we can usually expect one sitting in every four or five to be a bit sleepy anyway. The sitting then becomes like a short semi-conscious nap to revive yourself.

You could also meditate lying in bed with an alarm clock. The body is biologically designed to go into a rest phase, if not actual sleep, once every 90 minutes. If you make sure you wake after 20 minutes, you maximize the benefit of that resting phase without wasting the afternoon.

Whenever I go on retreat, I let myself snooze whenever I feel like it, the way a cat does. I set the alarm and meditate to drop into sleep quickly. I often wake before the alarm goes off 15 minutes later. I might do this four or five times a day. I find this keeps me fresh and dispels those sluggish patches. It also means I need less sleep at night and am able to get up about four or five in the morning.

WHAT IS GOOD BREATHING?

If we can 'just watch' the body and the breath, without trying to control them, they usually find their own way towards balance. But what is good breathing anyway?

When we watch the breath, we rarely find it is perfectly fluid and easy. Tension has the effect of inhibiting the breath. As we relax, these blockages start to loosen automatically. In other words, we don't have to 'do' anything to relax. Just noticing the tensions is enough.

Relaxed breathing is often quite erratic - now shallow, now deep, occasionally stopping. If you've ever noticed a healthy baby sleeping, you'll notice their breathing is rhythmic and flowing and luxuriously indulgent. No wonder we wish we could 'sleep like a baby'. But even this healthy breathing is still not perfectly regular. You'll notice the odd deep sigh and jerky patches, and times when the breathing stops altogether.

The same happens in meditation as you relax. This changeable breathing feels lovely, and yet it can be quite different from what we think of as 'good' breathing. It's loose and spacious, but not necessarily regular or deep. It is changing in response to subtle shifts within the body and mind. This is why you don't try to breathe deeply or regularly throughout a sitting. It inhibits the natural changes in the breath.

THE DESIRE TO CONTROL THE BREATH

Many people are quite anxious about the natural activity of their bodies. They wonder if they are breathing 'correctly', and feel they should control it to 'make it better'. Meditation, however, is not about control. It is about focusing and letting go, and trusting the body and mind will find their own way home if we stop trying to manipulate them.

Our tension often comes from the effort to control our bodies anyway. We may not realise how much we do this, since the habit builds over decades. Some people hold themselves very tight, attempting to dominate the uncontrollable. Others are more trusting, and sympathetically listen to the needs of their bodies. One person learns meditation because 'I want to *make* myself relax'. Others are willing to *let* themselves relax. The latter usually do better.

Even little children control their breathing. When faced with overwhelming or unacceptable feelings, they learn to choke them back by holding their breath. Emotions ride on the breath and tend to move up or down through the body. Anger and joy move upwards, for example, and sorrow and fear move down. The easiest way to suppress them is to cramp the breathing. The blockages most commonly occur in the throat, the chest and the diaphragm.

If the emotion never releases, the control has to stay in place to keep it down. We do breathe of course, but it's stiff and jerky, which is why many people find the breath quite uncomfortable to focus on.

Relaxation involves a letting go of tension and control. But if chronic anxiety and workaholism have got you where you are today, you are naturally reluctant to give them up. Your doctor tells you to take it easy, but your conditioning says, "Don't you dare! Your life will fall apart if you do!"

CONTROLLING THE BREATH CAN BE USEFUL

Ideally we just let the breath flow the way it wants. In practice, the blockages can be too strong to dissolve naturally, and controlled breathing can help loosen them. For example, you could do some yogic breathing exercises, or just try to make your breathing deep and rhythmic at first. Even simpler, you could take a few deep breaths and sigh at the start of any sitting.

Controlling the breath like this can focus the mind well, but it's still a control mechanism. It is good to go the next step and let the breath be free. Relaxing should be like sleep. We don't control the breath when we sleep. Nor do we need to control it when we relax.

Nonetheless, I find about a quarter of the population will always try to control the breath. It's just their nature. This is not a problem so long as they control it as little as possible, like gently holding the reins of a horse. It's quite okay to smooth the rough edges of the breath and round off the turns. In fact, when the breath becomes extremely fine in states of deep tranquility, it is actually hard to say whether we are controlling it or not.

Control is not automatically 'bad' and freedom 'good'. We need a little of both, though we tend to err on the side of control. Christianity emphasises man's dominance over nature, and though we may no longer be outwardly Christian, that attitude can still cast its shadow over us when we meditate. We may feel we should impose our will on the breath and the body, as if we can't trust them to do the right thing.

The Eastern assumptions are different. It is assumed that nature can be trusted, and that the body is wise. The human model has been around millions of years and it knows how to breathe. If we get our interfering mind out of the way, it will do exactly what it needs for health and balance. Good posture and breathing, and lovely states of mind, emerge naturally from within, if we let them. All we have to do is sit still and watch the process.

Spot-meditation: Sitting comfortably

The first few seconds of any meditation, however short, should involve fine-tuning your posture and breathing. It's an essential preliminary. This spot-meditation works with just this. At any time during the day, just notice how you are sitting and breathing. The awareness alone can have magical effects. Within seconds, you should feel the breath softening and muscles releasing.

INSTRUCTIONS

1.   You may be in an office chair or couch or on a bus.
      Stop whatever you are doing, and put the thoughts aside.
2.   Without changing posture, notice how you are sitting.
      Ask: "Am I more tense than I need to be?"
      You may feel it in the face or shoulders or toes.
      Also notice how you are breathing.

3.   Now adjust your posture. Do it slowly and deliberately.
      Listen to what your body wants.
      Make finer and finer adjustments.
      Go for a sense of balance and openness and comfort.

4.   When you feel 'in' your body, go to your breathing.
      Take three or four deep breaths and sigh.
      Now let the breath find its own rhythm - open, spacious and natural.

5.   Watch the process of the body returning to balance.
      Notice the little tensions surface and fade.
      Finally, resume what you were doing, staying aware of your body and your breathing.

Chapter eleven

Sound and Music

USING NOISE AS AN ALLY

Noise is an integral part of any meditation. Like the breath and the body, it is always with us. Any time we meditate, we'll inevitably be aware of sounds as well. We notice the traffic, the air-conditioning, a dog barking, a car-alarm going off, a door slamming nearby, a plane overhead and so on.

We may occasionally be oblivious to noise but it's impossible to block it out completely. For our safety, the mind is constantly hearing and identifying sounds. We can't switch this function off. It happens even when we sleep.

If you get annoyed and feel that sounds are disruptive, they will be. If you feel that silence is essential for inner peace, your meditation will always be vulnerable. You'll feel anxious each time you sit, and resentful towards the world that makes all that noise.

It's much easier if you feel at home with the soundscape and even use it to enhance your practice. After all, sounds are stimuli from the present. They needn't stir us up the way thoughts do. Listening to sounds is good for keeping the mind bright. It reminds you where you are and what you are doing. If you're getting sleepy in your meditation, you can become more alert by listening to the sounds around for a few seconds. If you lose the sounds completely, it's often a sign you're falling asleep.

When I sit, I periodically check my mental clarity by noticing how precisely I can listen. If the sounds are vague and blurry, and I can't quite catch the start of a new sound, it's obvious that my mind is rather dull. It's a sign that my attention is being drained by some semi-conscious thinking in the background.

MEDITATING DIRECTLY ON SOUNDS

Meditating on random sounds is an ancient practice and one of the best. One reason that yogis meditated in deep caves was to listen to the sounds of their own bodies. It is extraordinary how noisy we are - breathing, heartbeat, digestion, the hum of the nervous system and so on. Furthermore, this inner symphony changes its tune as we become more tranquil.

Sound meditations sharpen the mind. You have to pay moment-to-moment attention or you'll miss the next sound. Although the sounds are unimportant in themselves, when you're totally with a bird call or a car horn, the past and future vanish. When you start to notice the subtle sounds you'd normally miss, you know you're fully in the present.

Meditating on sounds can have quite a unique effect. It gives us a sense of space. Meditations such as the breath and the bodyscan have an introspective quality that takes us inwards. This can make us assume we have to withdraw from the world to relax at all.

Sounds, on the other hand, take us outwards. We may be focusing on things that are hundreds of yards away. The mind expands to encompass them. We also realise we can relax while being fully conscious of our environment. It's not hostile to our inner life. We only have to be passively aware and 'just listen' to it.

Random sounds give us a sense of space in other ways too. We hear one sound to the left and another far behind, and we notice the space between them. When you focus on a sound that vanishes, the mind is alert but empty. You are gazing into space. The same happens if it is silent and you're waiting for the next sound. You can be totally alert, though focused on nothing.

Soon you realise this sense of space and emptiness can be very stable. In time, it becomes a meditation object in its own right. When people talk about an empty mind, this is what they mean. It's not a mental blankness, since you'll notice the next sound immediately. It is in fact the pure consciousness through which all our thoughts and sensations pass. It is the featureless screen on which our mental activity is displayed. Focusing on sounds can give you your first real taste of this clear, spacious mind.

STRETCHING THE BASIC INSTRUCTIONS

We usually think of the 'meditation object' literally as a single thing. Focusing on random sounds seems to be stretching the instructions somewhat. In fact, the 'one thing' can be anything you choose to direct your attention to. In this case, it is the entire soundscape, which is made of hundreds of individual sounds. This practice resembles the bodyscan meditation, where you focus on many different sensations in succession.

Similarly, the 'meditation object' could be the sensations of swimming, or the activity of cooking a cake, or the storyline of a visualisation. Complex as these things are, they still have clear boundaries. When we meditate, we basically put a fence around the object and explore what is within the fence. When you notice you've jumped the fence and are chasing some thought, you stop and clamber back over the fence.

The fence could be huge enough to embrace the whole soundscape. Or it could be quite tiny - the breath at the point of the nose, for example. Random sounds are a good example of a large and varied meditation object. All that matters is that you know when you're inside the fence and when you're outside it.

MEDITATING ON MUSIC

Music is a natural thing to meditate on. It holds our attention well and leads us along in time the same way an instructor's voice does. If you lose it, it's easy to find it again. Being sensually rich, it draws us away from thought.

Yet there are problems with it. Few of us are used to listening carefully to music. We commonly use it as sound wallpaper, or drift along aimlessly with it, letting our thoughts go where they will. While this may be relaxing, it won't lead to mental clarity.

With any meditation, no matter how pleasant, there needs to be an element of discipline and self-awareness. You need to know what you're focused on and when you've wandered away from it. Without conscious focus, you won't be able to extract yourself from the habit of thinking. In this practice, you notice when you're really with the music and when you've gone off at a tangent.

Meditating on music should be like going to a concert. You can be relaxed but also alert. If you've paid $50 for a ticket, you want to hear what you've paid for. You don't want to space out for two hours. Fortunately, when you listen carefully, you find you enjoy the music all the more.

STAGES OF DEPTH

Any meditation will take you through stages of depth, and these are particularly obvious when we listen to music. At first the music seems to be somewhat distant and doesn't penetrate the cloud of our habitual thoughts.

Then the music breaks through and we tune into its mood. We may feel it in our bodies. Many people get images and associations, but none of these need to be a distraction. They are all part of the meditation object - i.e. the musical experience - unless you go off at a tangent with them. To check, you can ask yourself, "Am I still with the music?"

Just occasionally, we become so absorbed in the music that we are aware of nothing else. We forget ourselves and all our problems completely, for just a few seconds. This is when the music seems to become exceptionally beautiful. In fact, it's the mindstate that is beautiful. This is a state of oneness, or absorption, or what the Indians call 'samadhi'. Enjoy it while it lasts.

WHAT KIND OF MUSIC SHOULD I USE?

People often assume you need tranquil relaxation music to

meditate to, but this misses the point. It is the focusing, not the music, that does the work of getting the mind clear. It doesn't even matter if you like the music or not. After all, you don't have to like random sounds to use them as your focus.

Almost any music will do if it holds your attention. Recently a man told me that he meditates to the frantic jazz of John Coltrane. I also find that complex music, like Bartok string quartets, draws me in and keeps me focused well. The music you use could be fast or slow, tranquil or passionate, simple or complex, classical or New Age or planetary. It is your choice.

There are just two exceptions to this. Vocal music can get you thinking about what the singer is saying. And some New Age music is deliberately fluffy and insubstantial in order to make the mind space out. You need something clear enough to focus on, so you know when you've wandered away from it or not.

AMBIENT MUSIC

You can also use music to set a mood without actually focusing on it. In other words, you focus on the breath or whatever but with soft music in the background. Obviously, you will notice the music from time to time in much the same way as you notice random sounds, but it's not your main focus.

One advantage with ambient music is that when your mind wanders, it tends to fall into the music rather than into thoughts. The music acts as a safety net. The sensual and rhythmic qualities of music also tend to augment the sensory flavour of your meditation.

Unlike music you deliberately listen to, ambient music needs to be quite bland. Anything exciting or even musically interesting will distract you from the breath. CDs of nature sounds or relaxation music are quite suitable.

Finally, the music needs to be played very quietly - about half the usual volume. When we meditate, our hearing becomes very acute. The music should be so quiet that it doesn't dominate consciousness. It should be like the random sounds - something that you notice in passing and often don't notice at all.

Random Sounds

INSTRUCTIONS

Relax the body and the breathing as usual.
Tune into the soundscape.
Notice the background sounds you would normally ignore.
Don't reach after sounds. Let them come to you from all
directions. Follow sounds to the point where they vanish.
Try to catch a new sound the moment it arises.
Enjoy the texture and colour of sounds.
Listen to them as if they were music.
Enjoy the spaces between sounds.

Check your body to ensure you're actually relaxing.
Notice how simple this is: you're just listening. And when
thoughts arise, you acknowledge them and let them go.

Music

INSTRUCTIONS

Settle the body and the breath as usual.
Switch on the music and enjoy the colour and detail.
Let it resonate in your body.
If images or associations arise, blend them in.
Ask yourself occasionally, "Am I still with the music?"
Let the mind slow down and go into the fine detail.
Notice the special live quality when you're 100% there.
When the music stops, come back to yourself.
Did you relax fully, or are you still a little charged up?
Spend the last few seconds in silence.

Chapter twelve

Supporting your Practice

GETTING A PRACTICE GOING

In 1984, I did a seven-month retreat in ideal conditions. I was alone in nature with the freedom to do what I wanted. I had no books or media or other distractions apart from the internal ones, and I loved what I was doing. Nonetheless, I wondered how much my good results depended on the setting and the solitude. Would it all fall apart when I returned to the city?

Since then I've trained myself to be able to meditate anywhere, on anything, with anyone and under any conditions. I encourage my students to be equally versatile.

However, each week someone will say to me, "I can't find the time. It's really hard to do it at home" Or, "I know how to meditate, but I need to get into a routine again." Or, "I've been reading about it for years but I just can't do it."

Meditation is fragile. Because it is a quiet and subtle kind of non-doing, anything noisier in our lives can blow it apart. It needs to be tended well, like a young plant. It will easily die if you neglect it.

You've read this far, so you know what meditation is and how to do it. Your next step is the big one: doing it regularly. This is a challenge even for skilled meditators, but especially so for beginners. It will take imagination and trial-and-error to find what works for you amongst your other daily obligations. You will have to answer the following questions:

How much can I meditate?

When can I meditate?

Where can I meditate?

What will help me meditate better?

"HOW MUCH TIME DOES IT TAKE?"

Just because you've meditated in the past doesn't mean you can turn it on at will. Like any skill, it fades if you don't practise it and improves if you do. The wheels get rusty if you've missed even a few days, and your next session is likely to be ragged. If you get a routine going, however, it flows easily.

I suggest you aim for 15 minutes a day, five days a week as a minimum. You can do that in one sitting or in three or four short sessions during the day. If you do that amount you'll be happy with your progress. Any less and you'll find the stops and starts frustrating. It takes about two months for a beginner to engrave the practice in memory. Over that period, you really get to know what works for you.

For a formal sitting, 15 to 20 minutes is a good time. Of course, longer sessions are good too. You tend to go through three stages in any meditation. In the first stage the mind is chattering a lot. In the second, you relax rapidly and often get sleepy. In the third, you wake up a little and get the right balance: relaxed body and alert mind.

FINDING THE TIME

People often complain, "I haven't time to meditate!" One student said her life was too busy with full-time work and managing a family. She seemed so frantic I almost believed her. Halfway through the course, she gave up her job and suddenly had an extra forty hours a week. Yet she still complained, "I can't find the time".

We fill our lives with compulsive activity whether we need to or not. It is the keep-busy-and-worry habit gone crazy. A 15-minute gap will not miraculously appear in your day. We are too good at filling spaces up. If you want a long meditation, you usually have to schedule it in.

If you make meditation a daily habit, like brushing your teeth, it won't feel like something extra that you 'have to do'. Those few minutes help you function better, think better, sleep better and enjoy life more. They soon pay for themselves.

We don't have to carve a 15-minute hunk out of each day. In fact, there are gaps everywhere. The trick is to notice and use them. If you ask yourself repeatedly, "When can I meditate?", or "Could I meditate now?", you'll eventually find the spaces to do spot-meditations at least. These are the thin end of the wedge, giving meditation a foothold in your day. As one student said, "When I started doing the short meditations, they soon became longer."

"WHEN CAN I MEDITATE?"

There is no 'best' time to meditate. Is there any time of day you wouldn't benefit from being relaxed and aware? But some times will be more satisfying for you than others. The 'larks' amongst us like the morning. The 'owls' prefer the evening. Some times are suitable for short, but not long, meditations. Here are some of the common times that people meditate.

Very early morning is delightful. Monks and nuns throughout history have meditated in the darkness before sunrise. The body's metabolism is still slow but the mind is rested. This often gives a tranquil but alert meditation which lasts till the dawn. I find the early bird calls have an almost visceral effect on me, stirring me up for the day ahead.

Although pre-dawn is too early for most of us, early morning is still a good time, but do wake up first. If you try to meditate in bed, you will just go back to sleep. If possible, have a shower or brisk walk and then sit before the rest of the suburb comes to life.

After the rest from a night's sleep, we often speed up quite fast in the mornings. To come back into balance, it's good to meditate just before you leave the house. Three minutes on the couch is quite enough to reset the thermostat. Mothers often meditate just after the kids have left for school.

If I arrive early at a destination, I will sit in the car and meditate before getting out. One of my students says she deliberately leaves home early so she can do this at the end of her journey.

Many of my students who are business people will cut out 10 minutes in the middle of the day. They lock the office door, turn on the answering machine, and lie down on the floor or a couch. Others are more discreet, choosing to meditate in a park at lunchtime, rather than eating in a noisy cafe.

I discourage people from meditating while driving, though I know they do it. Beginners often assume that meditation is a sleepy, blanked-out state, regardless of what I say. Obviously, this can be dangerous while driving. People don't realise how rapidly they can drop from a state of relaxed alertness into unconsciousness. It only takes a few seconds asleep at the wheel to kill someone.

However, if you insist on meditating while driving, there are ways to make it safer. Don't use the breath meditation or mantra, which can be very soporific. Focus instead on the experience of driving. Pay attention to the scenery and passing traffic, and notice what you are doing. Notice your breathing and muscular tension, but don't go too deeply into them. In other words, stay present and in touch. If you emphasise this kind of scanning awareness rather than focusing deeply on one thing, you're likely to drive more safely and enjoy it more.

People often find it too distracting to meditate at home. It's better in their car. They pull over at a park or a beach on the way home and sit there, letting themselves unwind. One woman told me she goes out to the garage and sits in the car to meditate. "The quietest place in the house", she said.

If you meditate after arriving home from work, you leave work behind and reclaim the evening for yourself. It's often a messy sitting, as the remnants of the day straggle by, but it helps you detach from it all. It can act as a 'power-nap', giving you an energy charge afterwards. You find you can use your evening productively instead of crashing out in front of the TV.

If you sit before you go to bed, you won't take the problems of the day to sleep with you. But don't meditate too long. A long meditation will refresh you and you'll stay awake when you go to bed. 5 to 10 minutes is usually safe. Just get clear of the thoughts and catch that downward momentum towards sleep. Then go to bed.

Once in bed, you can meditate to put yourself to sleep. If you're tired, two or three minutes of good focus will usually send you off. If you wake in the night, you can meditate to go back to sleep. The secret is to meditate well. Listening carefully to music often works nicely.

Paradoxically it is best to aim for sharp focus if you wake at night. You can't waffle your way back to sleep. Good focus is what cuts you free from the thoughts that keep you awake.

THE SETTING

People who come to my centre often say, "I feel relaxed as soon as I walk in the room". Even experienced meditators appreciate having a specially designated time and place. It helps enormously to sit with others for an hour once a week, for example.

Because of the associations, people pick up non-verbal cues from the room that trigger off the feeling. It may be a smell, or something visual, or just the mind going through the memory bank saying, "I recognize this place. It's where I go into those nice inner spaces".

This will happen anywhere you meditate regularly. The sensations don't even need to be pleasant. The smell of mouldy carpet in the church hall where you sit on Tuesday nights could give you positive reinforcement.

Similarly, you may find that insignificant gestures have strong effects. For me, throwing my cushion into the centre of the floor was enough to change my living room into a meditation space. People often light a candle or incense. They put something beautiful in their field of vision, or have some very quiet music in the background. It doesn't take much to create a supportive mood. A hint is all you need.

Some people get more elaborate. They set up a small shrine with a candle, flowers, fruit and beautiful things on it. They then have a shower and put on white clothes, say a few prayers and go into the meditation proper. They often finish with some gesture such as blowing out the candle.

If you have a choice, it is best to meditate outside. Being in nature takes you away from the artificiality of modern life. On a beach or under a tree, the mind becomes more natural. To spend 15 minutes each morning on your verandah, consciously being in the present, would be a great thing to do.

EXTRA SUPPORTS

I encourage you to depend on yourself and be self-reliant. However, as a beginner, don't underestimate your need for support. There is no glory in struggling bravely on your own and failing. For example, at home you could play one of my guided meditation CDs to remind you what to do.

It's useful to sit regularly with other people. Many people say they meditate best in the 'energy' of a group. People who come together for a purpose tend to develop a collective mood that's like the sum total of all their moods mixed together. We're attuned to each other more than we think.

For example, the moment you walk into some offices you can feel the hostility and warfare in the air. It will affect your behaviour despite your best efforts. Conversely, a gathering of friends can have a positive atmosphere that can't be duplicated elsewhere.

As a result, a group of people sitting to meditate will tend to support each other unconsciously. Over time, you get an instinctive feeling for the flavour of meditation. I find most good meditators have spent at least a year or two associated with a group of some kind.

Lovely as a group atmosphere is, it often leads to dependency. People often tell me they can only meditate in a group. This tells me they actually don't know how to meditate. They are reliant on a certain mood that only occurs in that time and place. They often become dependent on the teacher as well. It happens very easily.

Religious groups deliberately exploit this tendency. They often create a beautiful, slightly hypnotic, atmosphere for people to feel good in without needing to meditate at all. Often they use props like singing, incense, lovely pictures, and meditations that 'guide' you, rather than 'teach' you.

The actual meditation component in a group experience can be quite slight. I am often appalled at the childish level of meditation instruction given in religious groups. Of course, it is not in their interests that you learn to meditate independently of them. Their survival depends on you being around as long as possible.

TALK WITH OTHERS

Part of the beauty of meditation is its solitary, non-verbal, inward nature. It becomes something unique to you. As a result, it's rare for meditators to discuss their experiences, even with their teachers. This is a big mistake. An intellectual understanding of the process is very valuable, and that happens best through discussion with others.

So use every opportunity you can to discuss your practice with others. Go to as many groups as you can to see what they do. This will highlight their similarities and differences. Get to recognise the nonsense and fluff that surrounds meditation, so you're not secretly awed by it. Learn to identify what is meditation, and what is just myth, promise, religion, advertising and magical ritual. And, of course, read books on the subject.

HOW DO YOU START? A SUMMARY

It's a big leap from meditating in a group or a class, or reading a book, to doing it on your own. It helps to consciously reproduce the supports of time, place and routine in your own practice.

First choose a time. It's great if you can schedule it in your diary. An even better approach is to ask yourself repeatedly during the day, "When could I meditate?" and try out various slots from early morning to late night.

Also ask, "Where could I meditate?" Just because your living room or balcony is an obvious place, don't get stuck there. If you ask yourself repeatedly during the day, "Could I meditate here?", you may find many unexpected places and times.

When you do a formal sitting, ask yourself, "What would help?" Very simple things such as burning an essential oil, or lighting a candle, or having a piece of music playing very, very lightly in the background can work wonderfully. Religious groups often sell you the incense they use in their temples for you to use at home. Just a single cue can be enough.

People often try to import the feeling of a class or temple into their solitary sittings in a devotional way. Hindus may put a photo of their teacher in front of them. Others will use a buddha image on a shrine. On a more modest scale, some of my students have imported me by reading an appropriate page or two of my book before they sit.

Even when you start to meditate, a routine is useful. Remind yourself what you're trying to do. You could just say, "I want to relax and settle the mind", or you could have a more personal goal. Don't just sit down blindly hoping something lovely will happen.

Traditionally, you're often encouraged to go through a set mental routine consisting of a prayer, a statement of aspiration and a bow or two. Personally, I don't find religious imagery helpful at all, but I do find value in a routine. I always scan the body and loosen the breathing as a preliminary for at least a minute or two. Only when I feel 'in touch' with myself do I decide what to do in that particular sitting.

Sanctuary

Many people complain they can't meditate at home because it doesn't feel like a meditative place (and it usually isn't!). But you can imagine being in some place that is much more suitable.

I like to tailor these escapist fantasies to my exact mood. I ask myself, "Where would I like to be, right now?" and wait for the images to arise. These are often quite precise and different each time. Perhaps I want to sit under the hanging branches of a tree in autumn, with evening mist around the hills. Maybe I want to be in the Arctic tundra in midsummer, or perhaps with my friend in New Zealand, having a cup of tea on his verandah.

In a good visualisation, each detail is like a holograph and contains the emotion of the whole. It's better to go deep into single details than to paint an entire picture. Imagine the smell of damp earth or the squawk of distant birds or the steam swirling from the teacup warm in your hands. Be as simple as possible and let the mind slow down. Let it stop if it wants to. Planning the itinerary for a trip through Europe won't have the same effect.

INSTRUCTIONS

Spend a minute checking the body and the breath.
Then ask "Where would I like to be right now?"
Select a place suitable for meditation, real or imagined.
Walk in and sit down, just like you're sitting now.
What is in front of your eyes?
What time of day is it?
What is the temperature and the weather?
What can you hear and smell and touch?
What is the mood of this place?
Very slowly explore your surroundings:
trees, sun, sand, clouds, birdsong, scent, breeze.
Focus deeply on a single detail, or on your breathing.
Enjoy being here.

Chapter thirteen

Watching the Stream
of Consciousness

WHEN YOU'RE CALM, YOU BECOME AWARE

When you're meditating well, your body and mind feel calm and still. And yet you'll notice the mind hasn't stopped completely. It's 'still' only in comparison to what preceded it.

Even in states of deep peace, you'll find that subtle images, thoughts, sensations and feelings continue to pass through consciousness. Furthermore, your experience is always changing slightly from second to second. This is what we call, for want of better words, 'the stream of consciousness.' It never stops and it's good to watch it.

When you're stressed, the stream is a raging torrent of unpleasant thoughts and emotions. When you're relaxed and still, however, the stream of consciousness becomes delicate and lovely and it doesn't disturb you at all. In fact, it's very useful to examine it. This is what you do in Awareness meditations.

Nonetheless, focusing come first and does the spade work. Focusing streamlines the mind like unifying the sun's rays through a magnifying glass. It takes you to that inner stillness where you can watch the mindstream while remaining clear of it.

The longer you stay in that space, the more exquisite and nourishing it becomes. It is deep, subtle, expansive and warm. You can feel all the systems in your body and mind becoming more harmonious and alive to a degree you never imagined possible. It's quite strange. There's nothing in there and nothing is happening. It's the inner sky. Yet it's also the most beautiful feeling imaginable.

You find it by going inwards. You move from the 10,000 things to the one. Once you find that inner stillness, however, it radiates back out to the 10,000 things. You can be calm and undisturbed in your core, as you go through your day. One part of you remains centred and still, though the rest of you is active. You've found the eye in the centre of the cyclone, or what a Zen teacher called 'the lotus in the sea of fire'.

BEING HYPER-PRESENT

When you're stressed, your compulsive thinking propels you through the past and future. When you're calm, you're finally free to be in the present. When you're perfectly clear, everything is just as it should be. You don't want to be anywhere else. There aren't any distractions. The mind is passive, alert and non-judgemental. You know what you are doing as you do it. You are now in a state of 'continuous clear awareness.'

Focusing is quite different from Awareness. Focusing fixes the mind on one thing. Yet it leads to Awareness, which is expansive and embraces the whole world. Awareness, as a practice, is commonly described in metaphors. It is said that the clear mind is vast and stable like the sky, with the thoughts and sensations like clouds floating by. Or that it is spotless like a mirror, reflecting all things equally and objectively.

The ideal is a serene, spacious mind, free of desire and aversion. Nothing sticks to it. It doesn't cling to interesting things or resist unpleasant ones. It is a 'choiceless' awareness, in that it doesn't value any thoughts or sensations more highly than others. It lets everything come and go in its own time. Though featureless, this state of mind is surprisingly beautiful in itself, being free of all disturbing emotion.

This is where you see things 'exactly as they are'. In this very moment, you know how your body feels, what your environment is, and what thoughts are in the mind. It all shifts a little in the next moment, and you monitor that too. You are 'passively alert' or 'witnessing' or 'just paying attention to what is'.

This leads automatically to self-awareness and insight. As you watch the stream of consciousness you get to know yourself in more depth. You see the raw data that actually makes up 'you'. This is the texture and contents of your mind. You become able to watch every last thought, sensation, feeling and image from outside, without trying to manipulate them.

You also see the causal connections: how a thought leads to a feeling which leads to a response in the body and often to action as well. You can often nip unhealthy thoughts and reactions in the bud, and foster healthy ones, and change your mood from frustration to peace instantly. You can bring the tensions and emotional imbalances to light and help them release. This is just one reason why awareness is worth cultivating.

Awareness really comes into its own at the edge of sleep. There is less emotional charge when you relax, so the mind is less 'sticky'. There is space between you and your thoughts. It is as if you've put the mind in neutral, and the gears no longer mesh with thoughts.

You often find here a subtle interplay of feeling, sensation, memory and thought that can be quite beautiful. You notice things you'd rarely notice otherwise: dream imagery, fluctuations in mood, inspirations and subliminal thoughts.

You're also awake enough to enjoy the profound pleasure of deep bodily relaxation, and the exquisite stillness and space of the mind itself. Of course, you 'watch it all dispassionately', but you can still enjoy it nonetheless. This is what keeps meditators coming back for more.

AWARENESS IS BUILT ON FOCUSING

Meditation involves both focusing (which leads to tranquility) and Awareness (which leads to clarity of mind). Some people, however, describe meditation purely as Awareness and regard focusing as a hindrance. Their instructions are 'just watch what happens' or 'watch the stream dispassionately' or 'just observe', but hardly anyone can do it this way.

It's certainly too much to expect from beginners. Awareness is almost impossible unless the mind is also anchored on a meditation object, usually the breath or the body. This tends to be so automatic with experienced meditators that they take it for granted. Usually, the sharper the focus, the sharper the awareness.

A saying illustrates this: 'Calm the mind down, then wake it up.' In meditation, you first emphasise tranquility and later shift towards awareness and insight. This is true both in a single session and over a lifetime's practice. Tranquility, which you get by focusing, is the roots of the tree. It grounds you in the earth of your own body and mind. Awareness is the trunk and branches, and insight, or self-understanding, is the fruit.

FOCUS AND RE-FOCUS

You need several strategies to develop good awareness. These change and become more sophisticated as the meditation deepens. Initially, you need to work hard to step outside the mindstream. Later, you can explore it at your leisure. Let me explain how these strategies work.

To escape the deluge of thoughts, you focus on a meditation object. This helps you turn your back on the stream. It's like having your hands on the steering wheel and your eyes on the road. When you lose focus, you inevitably fall back into the stream. So focusing is your first strategy.

Throughout the sitting, ask yourself, "Am I still focused?" Often you're caught in a chain of thought without even realising it. This happens more often than we like to admit, both in the meditation and out. So your second strategy is simply to re-focus when you lose it.

NAMING THE DISTRACTIONS

I hope you now understand the technique of 'naming the distractions'. In other words, when you realise, "Oh, I'm thinking about Sally", you say to yourself, "Sally". This gives you some detachment and the freedom to choose. You can often drop Sally on the spot. In fact, it's useful to know what's in the mind, whether it distracts you or not. It's good to acknowledge that Sally is shaping your mood in some way. This is to be aware of Sally's presence without letting her dominate you.

In practice, you don't have to literally 'name' things. It's quite enough to just see clearly what is there. Naming is a way of crystallising that insight, but it's too laborious and clunky to do continuously.

It's very rare to be 100% focused on the breath. A certain amount of mental scanning always goes on when we sit. Typically we may be 70% focused on the breath, and 30% monitoring the mindstream. This is why the instructions are in two parts: focus on one thing and just watch the rest.

So watching the passing thoughts is integral to meditation and it pays to do it well. You should be able to identify clearly what you're thinking about, whether it's annoying you or not. Awareness, after all, means seeing a thing 'just as it is', whether it's pleasant or not. The mind can be very calm and clear even while noticing a pain or a distressing thought.

Don't criticise yourself if you don't like the thoughts or the mood you're in. Awareness is more about accepting reality rather than escaping from it. And don't be afraid to ask the following questions while you meditate:

What am I thinking about?

(Or, what is grabbing my attention?)

What is happening right now?

(Or, what mood am I in? How does my body feel?)

SEEING THE IRRITATIONS WITH CLARITY

A huge variety of things go through consciousness. Some have a high emotional charge and some have a low one. It's easy to watch the pain of a slight headache. The pain of a bitter divorce is a different matter.

Each time something bugs you, you have a little challenge. Can you just 'see it as it is' and let go your aversion towards it? Can you passively watch, and indeed accept it? If you can't, your hostility keeps you tense. If you can, you will be calm and clear in the presence of something unpleasant. Meditation is very much about being at peace with things you don't like. A clear mind, by definition, doesn't get knotted up with likes or dislikes. The more you let them go, the happier you become.

Many distractions are sensory things, like noises or pains in the body. These don't need to be a problem. Being sensual, they keep you in the present anyway. If you notice a tickle in the throat or a plane going past, why not focus on them for the time they're there? You'll get much better at this over time.

Painful thoughts and feelings are a different matter. Being able to name the content of your thoughts - "Stephen, work, Paris" - will clarify most of them. However, you may also need to face the feelings behind them. If you chronically overeat, 'food' can be too superficial a word to identify what's going on. Or if you're worried about a drug-addicted daughter, saying 'Angela' doesn't encompass the matter.

So you could also identify the feeling behind a thought: 'despair', or 'desire', or 'contempt', for example. It's a big step to be able to say, "I'm thinking about money again and feeling sad and confused", but that is a moment of real clarity. Many feelings can't be caught in a single word, so it's usually enough to acknowledge the feeling.

Notice that naming the thought or feeling is not complicated. It's just putting single word labels on to the dramas. Also, you're not avoiding them, as you do when you try to focus on an object. Naming a thought is much cleaner than endlessly running stories around it. This saves energy and the body relaxes, even though the problem may not go away.

SHIFTING THE EMPHASIS FROM FOCUSING TO AWARENESS

There are many different aspects to Awareness practice. These include: noticing when you're distracted and re-focusing; identifying what's in the mind and freely watching the passing thoughts and feelings.

In fact, you practise Awareness every time you meditate. Whenever you 'just watch' a passing thought or sensation, or see what's happening just as it is, that's awareness. You may think you're just trying to focus but there's always an awareness element there as well.

What you do depends on how deep you go. At the beginning you have to get out of the stream, so focusing is critical. You keep your eye on the object. But once you're out and safely on dry land, the emphasis can now shift to Awareness. You observe what is actually happening in consciousness. While focusing never loses its importance, as people become more skilled, they tend to place more emphasis on Awareness.

Focusing keeps your eyes on the road, but Awareness lets you enjoy the scenery. Almost all the satisfaction of a sitting comes not from watching the road but from those sideways glances at the scenery. The physiological shifts, the bodily calm, the insights and the pleasure of mental freedom are all part of the scenery.

Awareness is a beautifully tolerant practice. Wherever you are, whatever you're doing, however you feel, you just see it as it is. Nothing is good or bad. It's all grist for the mill. Once you give up the vain striving, and the endless stories about the past and future, you discover how lovely it is just to be here.

Meditation is full of paradoxes. When you go into that still, lucid state beyond emotion, it is profoundly satisfying. It is a deep, all-pervading happiness that goes beyond wanting and having and getting.

And when the mind gets still, it doesn't go to sleep. It instinctively wants to explore and play, with a wonderful, childlike curiosity. This is the natural, ego-free activity of a calm and healthy mind, and Awareness meditations allow this to blossom.

AWARENESS IS A TECHNIQUE IN ITSELF

Awareness as a technique is most fully developed in the Buddhist practices of South-East Asia. It is commonly taught in ten-day intensive 'Vipassana' retreats. The word means 'insight' or 'mindfulness' or 'awareness' or 'seeing deeply' (into reality).

Of the thousands of meditation practices, almost all of them emphasise the focusing - going into a meditation object. The difference between them is what they focus on. Awareness, however, is in a different category altogether. This is because it emphasises the watching, not the focusing. And it can use any meditation object as an anchor.

Yet the instructions for Awareness are almost the same as any other practice: 'Focus on one thing and watch everything else with detachment'. It just gives you far more licence to watch. Though you may be anchored on the breath, your meditation object is actually the stream of consciousness itself.

At first, you simply notice the contents of the stream as they arise in consciousness. You don't search for anything. You just notice what walks in the door this moment, and the moment after.

Nonetheless, you may detect individual thoughts, sensations and feelings you'd never notice otherwise. It is usual to 'name' the main ones, but many are too subtle to name. And if you tried to name everything, you would be far too busy. It's quite sufficient to identify whatever is most obvious in the moment.

Neither thoughts nor sensations remain the same for more than a second or two. We can't take it all in at once, so we notice things serially. One thing after another catches our attention: "traffic . . . work . . . sleepiness . . . Peter . . . lunch . . ."

You can even ask, "what's happening here?" It is useful to notice a foggy mood, a mild headache, a sense of self-doubt, an array of small worries. Or tune into fleeting images or moments of subtle pleasure. Seeing it all without any desire or aversion, of course.

You don't go looking for things. You just wait, passive and still, for the next thought or sensation to come into view. It is like meditating on the soundscape, where you simply wait for the next sound. This keeps the mind sharp, and indeed 'aware'. It is remarkable what you will notice when you're not actively thinking.

If you're really calm and clear, you could even pluck something out of the stream and make it your temporary meditation object for a few seconds or a minute. You could focus on a dream image, or a mood, or a memory or a pain, for example. The usual instructions apply: focus on the (new) object and let everything go. This is using Awareness in order to investigate the mind itself.

Awareness

INSTRUCTIONS

1. Focus on the breath (or any other object) as usual.
Get a good grip on the object. Feel the body relaxing.

2. Now watch the stream of consciousness.
Ask, 'What is happening right now?'
Identify the most obvious thought or sensation right now.
Don't search for anything. Just notice what's there.
Enjoy the space if there seems to be nothing.

3. Notice how your experience is continually changing.
Every second, new thoughts and sensations come and go.
Watch it all dispassionately from the bank of the stream.
If you suspect you're falling in, you almost certainly are.

4. Don't lose focus on the breath.
It's your chair at the bank of the stream.
Spend half your time with the breath, half with the stream.
For stability, go as deeply into it as you wish.

5. Let the mind be open and tolerant, without boundaries.
Let go all effort, and the automatic likes and dislikes.
Don't try to change or understand anything.
Just be at one with the ever-changing present.

Chapter fourteen

Mantra

MANTRA IS A VERY SIMPLE PRACTICE

Awareness, the subject of the last chapter, is a sophisticated practice. Mantra is just the opposite. It is so simple that it is rarely 'taught' at all. You are usually told, "Here. Say this mantra". And that's all there is to it.

A mantra is a word or a phrase that you say over and over, often in time with the breath. It's a stripped-down form of chanting. It is like an affirmation, but affirmations have meaning and mantra often don't. Or the meaning they have is secondary to the musical effect of the sounds. Each mantra has its individual rhythm and sound quality, and people frequently sing them. This is often a sensual and slightly hypnotic practice to do.

Mantra is an exceptionally simple practice at heart. You say a mantra in much the same way as a little child will endlessly repeat a word to itself. Mantra often come with images and associations. These can be useful, or they could just clutter the mind. It is best not to regard a mantra as a magical or spiritual incantation. It is really just another thing to hold on to, like the breath.

Here are some common mantra:

OM

HAMSA (and its opposite, SOHAM)

OM MANI PEME HUNG

OM NAMAH SHIVAYA

HARE KRISHNA
OM AH HUNG

MANTRA CAN BE SAID IN MANY WAYS

Usually people say their mantra silently, or 'think' it, like an inner chant. They often blend it with their breathing to enhance its rhythmic qualities. A mantra is very easy to hold on to. Once you get a mantra ticking over, it becomes a soothing hum or resonance in the body.

Hindus often sing their mantra. Hinduism has a great tradition of popular sacred songs. People sing these for hours at a time, and the boundaries between mantra and devotional singing become indistinguishable.

People sometimes dance to their mantra, as we know from seeing the 'Hare Krishnas' in the street. Since it's hard to think of anything else while you do this, it is regarded as a good practice for young and undisciplined minds.

In India, mantra are often said very loud and fast. You occasionally see a holy man marching through the streets shouting his mantra. This is the high pressure hose theory of mantra. It blasts everything else out of consciousness.

People often start by saying a mantra out loud. As they relax, the mantra fades to a murmur. Then it goes silent and merges with the background hum of the body. Eventually the mantra stops of its own accord and the person rests in stillness. In the deepest states there should be no words at all, not even mantra.

Mantra and the breath meditation are the two most widely used meditations in the world. Most people have an immediate affinity for one or the other, though they frequently use both in time. The breath meditation is more cool, analytical and down-to-earth. It leads to clarity of mind. Mantra, despite the many attempts to demystify it, is still more emotive and hypnotic in effect. This is just the nature of mantra.

THE HISTORICAL BACKGROUND

The word 'man-tra' literally means 'mind-tool'. The 'tra' is actually the Sanskrit root of the English word 'trade'. It really is a tool for the mind to hold on to. It is a vehicle to take you deeper.

However 'mantra' also means 'a magical spell'. Of all the practices in this book, mantra carries the most religious and superstitious overtones. It comes from the abracadabra era of human thought when sounds were believed to have magical effects.

The earliest Indian texts we know of are basically collections of invocations and spells. The priests could say mantra to make the sun rise, the rains come, to protect you from disease, to destroy your enemies, to ensure the favour of the gods, to make your neighbour's wife fall in love with you, and in more modern times, to make your child pass his exams. Who said that meditation isn't useful?

Because the spells had to be said exactly right to work, a whole priestly caste emerged. They are the specialists in mantra and the associated rituals and sacrifices. We can be forever grateful to those brahmins who said the correct mantra this morning to make the sun rise.

The pseudo-scientific explanation for this is that each sound has a certain vibration that triggers off effects in our bodies and the world around us. As usual, there is a grain of truth in this. Sounds do have individual effects. The mantra 'Ah', for example, drops through the body like a sigh. If you said it thousands of times, you would become as loose as a beanbag. Though meaningless, it still has an effect.

The mantra 'Hoong', on the other hand, resonates in the chest like a bell, and holds in the energy. In contrast, the mantra 'Hree!' seems to shoot upwards and lift your energy. It is clearly not intended to relax you. Each mantra, therefore, has a different mood and effect which is amplified when you repeat it thousands of times.

Different religious groups often identify with a particular mantra. It is like their badge of allegiance or slogan. They also tend to claim special powers for their mantra.

Although mantra can be meaningless, they do tend to carry

associations. Tibetans use OM MANI PEME HUNG, which evokes one's sense of friendliness towards one's self and all living creatures. Siddha Yoga uses OM NAMA SHIVAYA, which evokes one's inner wisdom, symbolised by the god Shiva.

TRANSCENDENTAL MEDITATION

These associations can make mantra seem too religious or superstitious, so both Asians and Westerners have attempted to strip mantra back to its essence as a chant. Every culture uses chanting. Almost any word or phrase would suffice. You don't need one sanctified by thousands of years of use.

Benson in *The Relaxation Response* suggests using the word 'one' as a mantra. LeShan in his pioneering book *How to Meditate* suggests picking two syllables by opening the phone book at random. Rational as this seems, I find most people prefer the traditional mantra. There is something about their rhythm and sound quality that works well.

The Transcendental Meditation group (TM) came out of India in the late 1950s and set the benchmark for mantra practice in the West. They claim their practice is a no-nonsense psycho-physical discipline, and have helped enormously in making meditation respectable in the West.

TM is a very standardised practice. Every TM practitioner around the world meditates in much the same way, for the same period of time each day. Because of this, it is perfectly suited to scientific testing. Researchers love it. Most of the independent research on meditation has been done on TM for this reason.

Not surprisingly, it finds that meditation has many benefits. The TM people collect this research and use it to promote their product as scientifically proven. This is their main marketing strategy. However, they also go beyond the evidence to claim that TM is therefore superior, or 'transcendent', to all other practices.

In this respect, they are wrong. Most meditation practices have benefits that can be scientifically measured. However, comparative studies of the merits of different practices invariably fail to find any significant differences.

Despite its claim to be scientific, TM has cleverly exploited the magical associations of traditional mantra. Since each sound has a unique vibratory effect in your body, they argue you must use exactly the right sounds for you personally. They don't say what would happen if you used the wrong sounds. (Perhaps your liver would explode, or you'd go insane!)

Fortunately, they happen to be the experts in such things. For a few hundred to a few thousand dollars, they will give you your personalized mantra in an initiation ceremony. You are forbidden to tell it to anyone and you meditate on nothing else from that time on (unless you sign up for graduate courses).

So is TM a con? It has many features typical of a cult. It has an enlightened master at the top. It has its own metaphysical language and beliefs and residential communities. It operates in isolation as a world unto itself. It claims to be the one true way and is contemptuous of other practices. It sells a simple one-size-fits-all practice at a high price. If you sign up, you are encouraged to be faithful and, in fact, believe. And it has created a multi-billion dollar empire.

Nonetheless, the TM people are not pushy about asking you to take on the whole package. If you want to go further, you can. The TM people usually state that the meditation alone is sufficient. In this respect, they are more honest than many Buddhist and Hindu groups, who tend to give priority to ideology and belief.

Despite the hype, TM is just an ordinary mantra practice. It probably works well for that quarter of the population that is temperamentally suited to using mantra. It's expensive, but what price can you put on peace of mind? Many TM people have got their money's worth a hundred times over. If it's expensive, people are more likely to practise and therefore get good results. If they believe that TM really is special, this may activate the placebo effect so it could work well for them.

But do mantra need to be personalized and secret? After all, this is the only distinguishing feature of TM as a meditation practice. In the East, mantra are in the public domain. They are written on walls and printed on clothing and heard each day in the streets and temples. They're in popular songs, on the fronts of buses, engraved on rocks and fluttering from flags. Kids know them before they can read. There is even the reverse myth that the more people say a mantra the more powerful it becomes.

Millions of people are saying mantra this very minute. It is a very popular and effective practice. TM is out on a limb saying you need a personal mantra. It flies in the face of evidence, since personal mantra are rare in the Indian tradition. Millions of people over thousands of years have had excellent results using 'ordinary' mantra.

Most people who know anything about meditation look askance at TM's emphasis on a personal mantra. It looks like a marketing ploy to justify the high price. Usually the only people impressed by TM's claims are those who are new to meditation and who therefore have nothing to compare it with.

'HAMSA'

There are many two-syllable mantra. They fit the breathing easily: one syllable on the in-breath, one on the out-breath. Generally you breathe normally and let the syllables fit the length of the breath. If the breath is long you stretch out the mantra. If it's short, you contract it. If you try to breathe too regularly, you may hyperventilate.

HAMSA is a sensuous mantra. If you want, you can imagine the mantra (and the breath) like a wave, ebbing and flowing from your feet to your head and back again. You can imagine you are massaging the body with sound, or caressing pains and tensions in the body. First you say the mantra. Then the mantra takes over and carries you along.

If you just focus on the breath itself, you tend to notice the individuality of each breath rather than its rhythmic qualities. Mantra, however, make the breath seem more rhythmic. Like any rhythmic activity - walking, swimming, singing - this is soothing to the mind. It counteracts the restless, grasshopper nature of thought.

A mantra is just a meditation object like any other. The same rules apply: focus on the mantra and watch other thoughts and sensations with detachment. Occasionally, a mantra can have a hypnotic effect that makes you blind to your surroundings, but this isn't its purpose.

'OM MANI PEME HUNG'

The problem with two-syllable mantra is that as you relax and your breathing slows down, you can drift away - especially in that space at the end of the out-breath. The most famous mantra are usually longer and said faster. They give you more to hold on to, and usually have a good rhythm as well. They are commonly eight or ten syllables long, though some are thirty or a hundred syllables long.

Perhaps the most famous of all is the Tibetan six-syllable mantra, OM MANI PEME HUNG. It seems to consist of four little words, but it's usually said as a three-beat. The accents fall on the second, fourth and sixth syllables: 'Om-ma-ni-pe-me-hung.

The formal spelling is OM MANI PADME HUM and it is often pronounced this way. Meditators tend to blur the corners so it flows better. The mantra is usually said quite fast with no pauses and as a continuous patter, unrelated to the breath: 'Omaneepaymayhoong, omaneepaymayhoong, omaneepaymayhoong.'

This has a lovely rolling triple-time beat to it. It becomes a continuous flow of sound with an energising feel, quite unlike the ebb and flow of the breath. One student said it is like sitting in a train hearing the wheels go over the tracks.

It is possible to say this mantra in time with the breath, but few people do. It loses the forward momentum that is so much part of its character. I usually say it in time with the heartbeat. It is most commonly said as a continuous hum, independent of either heartbeat or breathing. It is like a bass note in your body - easy to hold on to and easy to return to if you lose it.

Tibetans commonly say it out loud but very quietly. If you go to a temple where there are lots of Tibetans, and hear a humming sound like thousands of bees, you now know what it is.

Tibetans will also say it while working or walking. One student told me of hearing it used as a work song. He was following porters carrying salt up a mountain. They were saying the mantra slowly, in time with their footsteps.

Mantra tend to have associations rather than meaning. This one is a 'heart-opening' mantra, designed to evoke a feeling of warmth and affection towards yourself and all living beings. The Dalai Lama is expected to manifest this mind state. It's part of his job description, and he does it well.

A visualisation associated with this mantra is to imagine your heart opening like a flower. From within the flower, the warm pink light of your affection permeates through your body, and then goes out to others.

Chapter fifteen

Affirmations

An affirmation is a word or a phrase that you say repeatedly through the meditation, often in time with the breath. It's like a mantra except that affirmations have meaning and mantra often don't. Like counting, this gives the mind something to do, so it doesn't wander off track.

Affirmations 'use a thorn to extract a thorn'. They use words to stop words. The continuous flow of sound can block the airwaves and stop other words taking over.

Here are some affirmations:

* PEACE
* RELAX
* SLOW DOWN
* LET GO
* LET IT BE
* BE STILL
* LOVE
* HAPPINESS

It is good to find your own affirmations. Any word or phrase that evokes a good feeling would do. If you enjoyed your recent holiday in Bali, you could use the word 'Bali'. The name of an absent lover or grandchild could suffice. A short phrase from a poem or a song would work equally well. The meaning isn't that important. Affirmations work because of their chant-like quality.

Affirmations can set a mood quickly. You add more colour to the breath meditation by saying an affirmation rather than counting. This can be like a mini-instruction, reminding you what you're trying to do. If you are getting uptight at work, just saying the words 'let go' a few times as you breathe could do the trick.

USING AN AFFIRMATION AS A CHANT

There are two very different ways of working with affirmations. You can say it like a chant or a mantra. Or you can use it as an anchor for contemplative thinking. The first will relax you more deeply. The second, however, can give you useful ideas.

Meditation is ideally a 'word-free' zone. Affirmations, however, are halfway between thinking and sensing. They do involve words and ideas, but very few of them, and they don't chatter on the way our thoughts usually do. Repeating a single word or short phrase hundreds of times has a chant-like effect that tends to squeeze unruly thoughts into the periphery.

Affirmations work well as a backup to the breath or to the bodyscanning meditations. In other words, you meditate on the breath but, instead of counting, you say an affirmation. This is like using an affirmation as sonic wallpaper or ambient music, rather than as a springboard for thought. It adds an encouraging mood, but it's not the main focus of the meditation.

So what kind of affirmation is best? A short or a long one? A simple one or a beautiful and spiritually uplifting one? It depends on what you want to do. Meditation works by streamlining your attention. In general, the simpler the practice, the deeper you go.

If you want to be calm and relaxed, then a simple affirmation will work best. At least the idea or the feeling behind it should be simple. Complex ideas and affirmations won't let you go into that space beyond words.

AFFIRMATIONS FOR CONTEMPLATIVE THOUGHT

Nonetheless, thinking does have a place in meditation. Buddhists say that insight and good ideas arise naturally from a tranquil mind. You don't even need to set the question, because the mind has an instinct to work on your deepest issues anyway. When the mind is calm, the answer comes.

Affirmations are often used as a vehicle for thought. In the Christian and New Age traditions, you relax and contemplate an inspiring idea, often with visualisations included. People will use affirmations to combat negative thoughts and reprogram their behaviour, as a kind of direct cognitive therapy.

However, people who try to evoke beautiful and useful thoughts often get indifferent results, particularly if they're anxious. When you're pursuing some thought for understanding or gain, there is bound to be some sense of 'I' and some kind of unfulfilled desire. This inevitably involves some tension and effort, and the process may be much the same as normal thinking. It's even worse if you regard an affirmation as an order from the mind to the body.

Because affirmations can be mentally stimulating, people often ignore the basics. However, if you don't do 'the boring stuff' of relaxing the body and calming the mind, then your thinking will just be a head trip. If you're deeply relaxed, on the other hand, the results can be wonderful.

'Thinking' while relaxed can put you in touch with deeper feelings and intuition. Rather than actively pursuing an idea, you can passively watch your mind revolve around it. It will be a slower kind of thought, with more lateral associations and unexpected insights. At the edge of sleep, you may even start 'thinking' in imagery and feeling as well as words. While not necessarily taking you to a conclusion, this strengthens the idea in your mind.

If you want to contemplate an issue by using an affirmation, it's usually best to crystallise it into a single word or phrase and say it silently to yourself. In this way it has the calming effect of a chant, while keeping you centred on your question.

The great mystic, St Benedict, said you should start with the word or phrase and then go to the wordless feeling behind it. You convert it from thought into feeling and finally embody it. This increased depth is often all you need to get a better perspective.

GETTING DOWN TO SPECIFICS

So what do you want to know more about? Peace? Love? Health? Happiness? Let's look at these. If you say one of these words with a question in mind, it makes an opening for something to happen. The secret is to simply deepen the mood in whatever way you can and wait for what arises.

When you say 'Peace', you are effectively asking 'What is peace?', and seeking the feeling. It's there. You know what it's like. You've been there before. You just have to keep your eye on it, and not get distracted. If you keep saying it, you'll recognise what undermines it and what strengthens it.

When you say 'Happiness', you are asking, 'What will make me happy?', both in this very moment and in the long run. Your body will eventually tell you what it wants, if you listen. Hopeful fantasies about the future may just make you restless and dissatisfied. Happiness could be more accessible than that. You may also see that happiness is always relative, and can't be nailed down, despite your best efforts.

When you say 'Health', you are asking 'What makes my body feel healthy?' You may realise that health is a feeling of ease and balance in the moment, and that your planning mind is disturbing that. If you keep your eye on the question, you may have insights about how your actions are affecting your health.

'Love' is a rich thing to meditate on. We talk about it a lot, but often in abstract terms. What does it actually feel like? A sense of warmth or flow or ease? A strain or longing? Is it on the surface or mostly hidden? Does it come and go and sometimes get lost altogether? What is the feeling of being loving towards yourself? Do you feel love differently towards different people? Finally, you ask, 'What kind of love do I want?' and imagine what that would feel like.

If you meditate frequently on peace, happiness, health and love, you'll actually know what they mean to you. You'll know what your body feels about them. They won't be just concepts and you won't get trapped in the words you spin around them.

Meditation also moves into the spiritual or philosophic dimension. Do you know who you are? Well, of course you do, but when you look more deeply, your sense of self often becomes evasive and fluid. The deeper questions arise: 'Who am I?'; 'What do I want?'; 'Where am I going?'; 'What is consciousness, or God, or the soul?'

It's clear that we're often unhappy because we haven't a clue how to answer these questions. These are often the reasons we go into meditation or an inner path in the first place. It's very useful and very Zen to hold such questions consciously, almost silently, in the mind, and wait patiently for the answers.

GOAL SETTING

Positive thinking, creative visualisations, believing in yourself and going out and getting it are a very American way of meditating. It goes back to the 1800s. It relates to that urban myth than any poor immigrant can arrive at Manhattan Island and become a millionaire if he believes he can.

So you set up an ideal and work towards it. You make it as real in your mind as you possibly can, even using visualisations to help you. You picture the ideal job, the ideal mate, where you want to be in five years' time, and the steps along the way.

There is no doubt this quality of focus is typical of many successful people. They don't blunder along hoping nice things will happen to them. They go into the supermarket of life with their shopping list worked out. This does help.

The negative side of this is that you can live in fantasy and inflation. Our thoughts don't create our reality. They only shape it somewhat. Having a dream and following it doesn't mean it's going to happen, no matter how beautiful the dream. If you live in fantasy and hope, you can get badly hurt when you're brought down to earth. And if your only strategy is to fantasise some more, you could be in real trouble.

Goal-setting affirmations work best to reinforce something that is already happening, and to remind you what you are doing. They can't materialise things out of thin air. To use a simple example, if you say the word 'peace' when you're in a state of panic, it probably won't work. But when you start to relax, and the first traces of peace are visible, then the affirmation will strengthen them.

So, to summarise, if you want to relax deeply, then use an affirmation in a simple, chant-like, almost mindless way. If you want to contemplate an issue, then it still helps to relax as deeply as you can first. Then hold the question in your mind, and passively notice thoughts and associations arising around it. Give it space and let your instinct or the deeper, wiser part of your mind do the thinking for you.

Affirmations

It is easy, though not essential, to combine affirmations with the breath meditation. Single word affirmations are usually said on the out-breath. Two-word affirmations obviously fit the in- and out-breaths. Even longer affirmations can usually be woven into the breathing.

INSTRUCTIONS

1.   Settle the body and let the obvious tensions go.
      Feel the ebb and flow of the breath within you.

2.   Say an affirmation as you breathe.
      Let it blend with the natural breathing.

If the breath is short then shorten the affirmation.
If it's long, then stretch it out.
Enjoy the chant-like, slightly hypnotic quality of this.

3.   Feel the body relaxing and the mind settling.
        Let the affirmation set the mood like ambient music.

4.   Contemplate the affirmation if you wish.
        What kind of feeling does it evoke in your body?
        Allow associations, images and feeling to arise around it.
        Don't get too active. Stay in touch with the breath.
        Make sure the body remains passive and open.

Chapter sixteen

Shifting into Alpha

When you meditate, you may notice that certain thoughts are like the tail that wags the dog. They affect your body instantly. Exciting or anxious thoughts stimulate the fight-or-flight response. They act as stimulants, putting us on red alert. Other thoughts are like sedatives, dissolving tension immediately.

We can escape the effect of stressful thoughts quite easily, and we don't have to formally meditate to do so. It can happen within seconds. You only need to shift from thinking to sensing, or from thoughts of the past and future into the sensations of the moment. Or, to put that another way, you shift your brain wave activity from beta to alpha.

BETA AND ALPHA BRAIN WAVES

When we relax, the electrical activity in the brain changes. While you can't see this unless you're wired to an electroencephalograph, it's good to know about it. When you are thinking, the brain emits what are called *beta* brain waves. These are between 14 and 30 cycles per second, and they look like choppy water on a graph. Their agitated jumpy lines even look like the way we think.

When we relax or are in sensing mode, the brain waves settle down. They become bigger, slower and more rhythmic. They look quite lovely and even serene on the graph. These are called *alpha* brain waves and are between 7 and 13 cycles per second.

In the beta state we think. In the alpha state we feel and sense things. In beta we are tense and burning energy. In alpha we are relaxed and conserving energy. During the day we alternate beta and alpha. We need both, but we tend to overdo beta and ignore alpha.

Beta is not all bad. It is an active, responsive state of mind. We are in beta most of our waking day. It enables us to think, talk, handle many different stimuli at once and speculate about past and future. It is associated with the left side of the brain which handles analytic, linear, critical thought. We need beta. It gets things done.

Nonetheless, beta activity is usually powered by low-grade fear, anger or desire. You may be afraid things won't work out, or angry about what is happening. Or you really want something to happen. This is our everyday, self-oriented drip-feed of fear, anger and desire.

This is exhausting and burns out the energy reserves. At some point we feel tired and start thinking about a tea-break. The mind naturally wants to drop into alpha - the relaxed, sensing, passive state - to rejuvenate itself.

If we ignore this impulse, the mind often switches off anyway. Despite our drive and extra cups of coffee, the fatigue sets in. We go into mentally blank patches for minutes at a time - often about late morning or two o'clock in the afternoon - before recovering somewhat.

SHIFTING VOLUNTARILY INTO ALPHA

The alpha state is the natural antidote to a busy mind. When we feel tired and can't think well, then alpha is reappearing. When sensing outweighs thinking - when biting into an apple or listening to rain, for example - we are shifting into alpha. When we feel an emotion in our guts rather than verbalizing it, we are in alpha.

Alpha is a state of 'being' rather than 'doing'. It is intellectually simpler but more grounded than beta. You may not sparkle verbally in alpha, but you know where you are and how you feel. If you check, you'll also realise the body is less aroused and you're burning less energy.

We can switch between thinking and sensing very rapidly. When talking to a friend you will be in beta. If you simultaneously try to listen to music in the background, you won't be able to get into it. Your brain is in thinking, not sensing, mode. But if you said, "Let's listen to this song", the difficulty would vanish. Within a few seconds, your brain could shift into alpha and enjoy the music.

We don't need to sit for half an hour a day in formal meditation. That's just practice. It is like doing the scales and never playing the music. All we need is to spend less time thinking and more time sensing.

Being more sensual can also make you happier. Meditators in general are happier people not because they've found peace, but because they enjoy life more. They have more gaps between the thoughts. They taste their food, feel the morning wind on their faces, notice the sunset and enjoy the touch of another person a little more than most.

AN ESCAPE FROM WHICH REALITY?

People sometimes ask, "Is meditation an escape from reality?" Certainly when we relax into alpha, the world looks different. If to 'be in touch with reality' is to worry about things that haven't happened, to fret over things that can't be changed and to react with panic to daily events, then the answer is, "Yes. Meditation is an escape from all of that".

A person who is chronically tense will see the world through the beta state of mind. This is the reality of money, work, superannuation, getting the kids through school and the Gross National Product. It is fueled by unresolved fear, anger and desire. We can live entirely in this state if we want. We could call this an active, thought-dominated, 'male' reality.

A person who can easily relax, however, sees the world differently. In alpha, the concerns of the past and future fade. We are more alive to sensation and feeling. We feel okay where we are and don't anxiously long for things to be different. We could regard this as a passive, sensation-dominated, 'female' reality. When we stroke a cat or enjoy an apple, are we really 'out of touch with reality'?

When we fall asleep, we enter yet another reality. Dreams are real to us when we are in them. Are they a complete illusion just because they don't match waking reality? So which is real? The beta or alpha or dream perspective? And is one more important than the others?

Because meditation enhances alpha reality, this can be disturbing for people who operate on adrenalin. They can't imagine being relaxed while awake. It is as if their bodies only have an on/off switch, and relaxation can only mean sleep and oblivion. In class, I see such people collapse into the sleep zone within seconds of starting to relax.

If you suffer from high anxiety, you may even feel it is dangerous to relax. The fight-or-flight response, after all, is the way you cope with challenges. If you relax at all, you may feel your life will fall apart. Some people even suffer what is called 'relaxation-induced anxiety' if they let their guard down too much. Being relaxed is unfamiliar territory for such people.

USING MEDITATION TO ESCAPE

In fact, some people do meditate and turn to a spiritual path to avoid facing their problems. When people can relax deeply, they often resent returning to the outer world. They feel the demands of children and work are undermining their spirituality. "If only I could meditate all day", they think. "If only I could go to India and be with the Teacher always. . ." Or, "If only I could lead the pure life, I would progress inwardly".

This antagonism towards ordinary life is encouraged by many religious groups both East and West. Cults in particular encourage an infantile dependency among their followers and demonize the world outside their community.

Even at the micro level of a single meditation session, some people try to escape reality. Although meditation should be an alert state, as you relax deeply it can be hard to stay awake. Some people enjoy this lack of clarity and get good at sitting in a torpor. They don't quite fall off the chair, but they are barely there. It is a calm state, which is why they enjoy it, but also anaesthetized and rather dull.

Some meditators get stuck in this state for years. They say things like, "I can switch my mind off whenever I want to". Or they feel good if they space out for half an hour without knowing where they are. It looks good but nothing is happening. It is one of those seductive side-alleys that meditators can get stuck in.

Even good meditators can have a sneaking fondness for oblivion and actively seek it at times. And in fact it's not a bad thing to do occasionally. It is quite healthy to be this relaxed, and often it's all you're capable of at that particular moment. It's a good place to visit but a waste if you go there habitually.

MEDITATING WITH EYES OPEN

To stop my students getting addicted to drowsiness, I suggest they meditate occasionally with their eyes open. I look for this as a sign that tells me a student is maturing. I notice them occasionally opening their eyes for a minute or two during a meditation to counteract sleepiness. Or I find them doing a whole meditation with eyes open. Or they sit comfortably for the first or last two or three minutes with their eyes open. I know these people really understand that meditation is 'a relaxed and *alert* state".

Many people find this idea absurd at first. They say, "As soon as I open my eyes, it's all over". They feel it's impossible to relax unless they shut the world out and fall into a fuzzy torpor.

Others want to know why they should be able to meditate with their eyes open. "It's so much easier with my eyes closed," they say. Many come to classes simply to relax, and it is a real achievement for them to do so quickly and consciously. It's invaluable for insomniacs and for those who suffer extreme anxiety and for those who want to switch their minds off.

Nonetheless, there is a long list of reasons why open-eyed

meditation is good. Firstly, you can meditate anywhere, anytime and no one notices. You can calm the body and mind while in a bank queue or a boring meeting or a waiting room or on public transport, or while walking or doing exercise or housework. If you have to keep your eyes closed to meditate, your possible times and places are very limited. It remains something you have to do in private, like getting undressed or going to the toilet.

Secondly, you realise that meditation is not a secretive inner state that only grows in seclusion. Open-eyed meditation counteracts the navel-gazing tendency and vague hostility towards life that meditators can fall into. Once you know how, you can de-stress and return to a calm, clear state at any time during the day. In fact, life isn't Hell. It's just a matter of how you respond to it. You don't have to escape to feel good.

Thirdly, you can meditate on things of beauty. Flowers, candle flames and crystals are common things to choose. In the Asian tradition, you could also focus on a tree, clouds, the wind in the grass, the colours of a sunset, a bird in the scrub, sunlight sparkling off water, a dead leaf, a spider web or the night sky.

This increases our sense-pleasure and empathy with nature. We see more deeply into things. People often say things like, "I don't think I've ever looked so deeply before at a rose (crystal, flame, driftwood, apple, blade of grass. . .)" The fine-grained detail of life emerges and a new world unfolds.

Fourthly, your meditation practice can become much more interesting. Meditating forever on the breath can get tedious. A lifetime focused on just one thing is not good. The chaotic mind does needs discipline, but we don't need to be masochistic about it. Meditation should not be a state of penitential boredom.

Fifthly, being able to meditate on different things means you do understand what meditation is about. Many groups and traditions want you to focus on just one thing forever. They say, "this mantra has a superlative effect. Nothing compares with it." If you feel you have to use just this mantra or only the breath in a certain way, it keeps you dependent and can lead to exploitation.

But meditation is not about focusing on the breath or a mantra or any one object. It is about focusing as a skill in itself, and you should be able to focus on anything. It is about directing your attention where you want it to go, both in the meditation and out. This is what settles the mind and sharpens your vision.

THE BENEFITS OF WAKEFULNESS

Each meditation has an after-effect. If your meditation is relaxed but foggy, that fogginess can continue. You find you're just 'not there' for several minutes afterwards. While closing your eyes and relaxing is useful, it's even better if it leads to a clarity of mind. A clear mind is like having clean spectacles, and this effect lingers after the meditation is over. You can calmly and deliberately see what is happening around you and act appropriately.

People say things like:

"When I come in here after work I never notice the park. But when I leave, the trees look so alive and beautiful."

"I always study better after meditating."

"After I meditate, all my senses are heightened."

"For the first time, I could see what was happening between me and my daughter."

Meditation changes our lives for the better not just because we relax more and sleep better. It is because we wake up and see what is happening. We are in touch with the physical sensations and emotions of being alive. This is what we call 'awareness'. For better or worse, it puts us in touch with reality.

Spot-meditation: Going to the toilet

It's quite relaxing to go to the toilet. At least one sphincter has to relax completely or it's not worth going there at all. And when you let one muscle go, others can relax in sympathy. Furthermore, the toilet may be the only place all day where no one will disturb you.

The Buddha was the first person to recommend urinating as a meditation object. This is a practice that is at least 2500 years old. A psychologist friend reminded me of this recently. He says he goes to the toilet in the five minutes between clients, and lets *everything* go along with the urine. He gets so relaxed in those few seconds he says he can barely hold his balance.

In Western literature, it is surprising how often the toilet is regarded as a suitable place for deep thought. You sit down and settle into your body. You relax and wait, and randomly survey the state of the nation. Not surprisingly, bright ideas can pop up and you feel relaxed for minutes afterwards. An excellent meditation!

INSTRUCTIONS

As you approach the toilet, get out of your head and into your body.
Feel the pressure in your bladder.
As you urinate, close your eyes and sigh deeply.
Feel all the muscles of the body loosening in sympathy.
Don't hurry to finish.
After the last drop, stay motionless for a few seconds more.
Walk away with a smile on your face.

Chapter seventeen

Meditating on Visual Objects

It's good to be able to relax with your eyes open and do 'spot-meditations' anywhere, and at any time. Just a minute is enough to drop your tension levels maybe 20%. If you do this several times a day, the cumulative effect can be huge.

You can, of course, focus inwardly on the breath, even with your eyes open, but it's more natural to choose a visual object. It is surprising how often we find beautiful things right in front of us - a flowering bush, storm clouds, a bright design on a dress or book, the grain of wood on a table. Otherwise, a spot on the carpet or someone's shoe will do just as well.

You can also do this practice formally, as is done in the East, by setting up an object at the right distance in front of you. In the instructions below I will give you lots of options to play with. Please adapt them as you wish. The bottom line is: enjoy what you're looking at and relax.

WHAT HAPPENS WHEN YOU FOCUS ON AN OBJECT

I usually teach this meditation by putting several objects on a low table - some flowers, a candle, a mango, a piece of driftwood, a silk scarf. Some students are interested in none of these, and focus instead on the table or the carpet (which are also quite attractive).

Even a visual object meditation should start with adjusting posture and loosening the breath, if only for fifteen seconds. I then ask the students to let their eyes roam casually over the objects until something leaps out at them. Once they've made their choice, they let their gaze settle into it.

When we are mentally active, our eyes are continually moving in their sockets. They move faster when we are tense and slower as we relax. It is not surprising that the little eye-swivelling muscles feel tired at the end of a day. This eye movement is also what keeps things in our peripheral vision in focus.

Nonetheless, it's easy to consciously soften the eyes and let them settle on one thing. Once the eyes soften, the whole face can soften in sympathy. You let the eyes blink as much as they want, so you're not staring.

Now you slowly and gently take in your object. You observe colour and shape and texture. You let your eyes go for a lazy stroll over the object and bring up the photographic detail you didn't notice at first. In other words, you're not blankly staring in the hope that you'll relax. If someone asked you what your object looked like, you could tell them.

When they do this practice in the East, they sometimes 'name' their object. In other words, you could say 'rose' each time you breathe out. If you're more tuned into the colour than the object itself, you could say 'red'. In fact you could do both, and say 'red' as you breathe in and 'rose' as you breathe out.

This connects your body and the object. It's as if you're breathing through the object. The words act as an affirmation, reminding you what you are focused on. This device is particularly good if you are in a place with lots of distractions, such as a supermarket queue.

When you relax, you occasionally get optical distortions. Often your peripheral vision goes hazy, or you get a tunnel-vision effect, or the carpet starts to swirl. This occurs because your eyes are not moving around as they usually do.

The eyes actually have to move slightly for us to see anything at all. If they become utterly still, as can happen in a deep meditation, you actually see nothing at all although your eyes are open. You're so tranquil that nothing matters, but a little voice within you asks, 'Am I going blind?'

Paradoxically, you can relax rapidly with your eyes open. I think this is because you know immediately when you've lost focus. Also, a visual object can be easier to return to than the breath.

When we relax, our imagination often comes to the fore. Just as listening to music can raise images and memories, so can looking at an object. You look at a flower and remember your grandmother had similar flowers in her garden. You look at a mango and remember the taste and texture of the last mango you ate.

When I was a child, I used to imagine what an ant would see as it climbed a tree. If you want, you can imagine climbing over an apple, or going inside it. You may look at an odd-shaped rock and see an elephant there, or a face looking back at you. If this happens, then have fun with it without getting too excited. Meditation should have an element of play about it.

You'll find that focusing on a visual object can relax you very rapidly. Within three or four minutes, you may find your eyes wanting to close. If you do so, you'll realise how relaxed you've become. You're often just one step above sleep.

You can even close your eyes, and continue focusing on an object by going over it in your memory. Very few people see it vividly, as if it was projected on a screen, but we can all remember something about it. Just to say the words, 'red rose' as you breathe would be quite enough to keep you focused.

TAKING A SNAPSHOT

If you look carefully at anything, you'll find you can bring it to mind later in the day. For example, I can still remember the little white chihuahua I saw as I walked to the supermarket this morning. The usual reason we can't remember things is that we didn't notice them in the first place. Our minds were too cluttered to take in anything else.

I love to meditate for short bursts on visual objects. I call this 'taking a snapshot'. I aim for a few seconds of total absorption in a leaf, a bird's feather, the bark on a tree, or a shadow on a wall. The 'exposure' may only be five seconds, but it cuts the other thoughts dead. In those few moments, I've lost myself. I'm just leaf. I'm just chihuahua.

I often do this while walking. I pass a cat on a brick wall and imprint it in my mind. As I walk on I play over the memory of the cat for the next half minute or so. It is extraordinary how much detail you can catch in a flash.

At the end of the day, it is easy to bring some of those snapshots back. If I am meditating, I can pull one out and focus on it for a few seconds. It is like reliving the loveliest moments of the day. In fact, I can still remember snapshots from years ago. Taking snapshots like this enhances memory and is a good training ground for visualisation.

The traditional Buddhist training had you look at a lotus in front of you. You would then close your eyes and picture it. When you lost it you'd open your eyes to look again, and so on. By the end of the day, you could walk through the forest with the lotus comfortably lodged in your mind.

Visual Object

INSTRUCTIONS

1. Spend a few seconds relaxing your body and breath.
    Settle your eyes on something in front of you.
    Let your gaze soften.

2. Slowly and playfully examine your object:
    colour, shape and texture.
    You could name the object or the colour or both, as you breathe.
    Use your imagination if you wish. Imagine touching or going inside it. If associations arise, weave them in.

3. Close your eyes and go over the memory of the object.
    It usually helps to name it as you breathe.
    It doesn't matter if the object changes slightly.
    Meditate with your eyes open or closed as you wish.
    Open them if you're too dreamy. Close them if you're tense.
    Check your body to make sure you're not trying too hard.

Chapter eighteen

Walking as a Meditation

You don't need to sit down to meditate. Almost any meditation you do sitting can also be done walking. Any good meditator should be able to get off his chair or cushion and stay calm and relaxed while walking.

Even experienced meditators assume that if an hour of sitting meditation is good, then four hours is that much better. In fact, too much of a good thing turns it into a bad thing. Too much sitting can lead to torpor and excessive introspection, and a desire to retreat from the world. It's rarely good for people with depression, for example.

If we only think of meditation as the deep tranquil state we get while sitting, then we can't integrate it into our lives. Our physiology changes when we start moving. This doesn't mean we're stressed, but the feeling is not like the low metabolic state we're in while sitting. Nonetheless, we can still be calm and clear-minded while active, even if it has a more awake quality.

For some people, walking is by far the best way to meditate. It particularly suits those who are young or mentally active or highly stressed or anxious. For these people, sitting still just doesn't feel right. They can force themselves to do it, but they'd do much better walking.

If you sit to meditate, all your worries can jump on you. Once you close your eyes, you may find yourself caught in thought from start to finish. It could be much easier to relax by taking a dawn stroll by the river or an evening ramble through the back streets.

The fight-or-flight response fires up the body for action. This is why, when you're under stress, you unwind better by being active than by sitting. It's what the body wants to do anyway. Sitting still can just make the muscles lock up further.

The body enjoys moving. Parents use it to soothe their babies. Walking is rhythmic and anything rhythmic stimulates the alpha brain waves. It moves the juices along and keeps muscles and brain alive. If we are too sedentary, the muscles atrophy and the mind feels dull. The continuous ripple of sensations can massage the muscles made tight by too much sitting or thinking. If we stop moving altogether, parts of the body start dying, and that doesn't feel good at all.

Walking takes you into neutral territory. You can metaphorically walk away from home, work and responsibilities and leave them behind you. Walking simplifies things. You can't do much else when you walk. But it does put you in touch with yourself, your body and the natural world.

AN ANCIENT AND VERSATILE TRADITION

Walking meditations have an ancient history. It is sad they're largely ignored now. Perhaps this is because few Western teachers have been thoroughly trained, and most Asian teachers are too encumbered by religious obligations to be good instructors.

Walking is as traditional a meditation posture as sitting. The Indian holy men and women of old weren't monks. The monasteries came later. They were pilgrims, or 'wanderers' or 'homeless ones', who brushed the dust of city life from their feet and roamed all their lives. Walking reminds us of our nomadic ancestry when we owned nothing and faced each day afresh. A simple life.

The Buddha encouraged his students to spend no more than three days in one place (except during the rainy season). So they walked a lot, and developed walking into a deliberate practice.

Over the years, these simple practices became elaborate and formal. Burmese monks may walk extremely slowly, verbally noting each micro-movement of the feet. It can take half an hour to cross the room, walking like this. While not that relaxing, it can make the mind exceptionally sharp.

Zen practitioners may walk together in a circle, synchronising their steps. Kung Fu and Tai Chi are elaborate versions of the Buddhist and Taoist walking and standing meditations.

On some ten-day retreats, people alternate sitting and walking meditations. It is traditional to walk slowly back and forth on a path about twenty yards long. Sitting and walking complement each other well. Sitting makes you calm but a little dull. Walking makes you sharp but is not so relaxing. So you walk to wake up and you sit to settle down.

Yet I think that ordinary walking, like ordinary breathing, is best. It's also more versatile. You can meditate any time you're on your feet - going to the shops, through the park, in a crowded street. Since you can't do much else while you walk, why don't you take it easy and get the mind clear?

SOFTENING THE EYES

Obviously, when you walk you notice people, kerbs, cars, trees, sky and birds. Our eyes usually hop from attraction to attraction like summer flies. If your eyes move too quickly, you won't relax much. You need to slow them down. There are several ways to do this. In all of them, the eyes will be active enough to stop you bumping into strangers and tripping over kerbs.

First you could hook them on a point in the distance - a car or tree - like casting a fishing line, and reel yourself towards it. This helps you resist the sideways glances. When you get too close, then cast your eyes over something else.

Secondly, you could look at the ground a few yards ahead. You can see where you're going but not much else. This makes you look quite serious and even pious.

Thirdly, you can let your eyes glaze over slightly. Let them rest back in their sockets and half-close the lids. Try to evoke the way the eyes feel as you come out of a sitting meditation: soft and gentle and even a little out of focus.

IT'S STILL A DISCIPLINE

One problem with walking meditations is that they're too pleasant. Because you feel good and there are lots of potential distractions anyway, you forget they're a discipline to help you withdraw from thoughts. Soon you're just walking in the park, with your usual mental cocktail of thoughts and feelings.

There are a few things that can help. It's good to be grounded in the body, even if you're primarily focused on something external. Also, encourage the mind to slow down. Although it's okay to shift your focus, unless you stay with each object for at least ten seconds, the meditation never gets going.

There are a huge variety of walking meditations. In the examples below, you'll notice the first three have you focusing inwards, on the body and the breathing. The later ones have you focusing outwards, on the sense world around you.

The boundaries between these meditations can easily blur. Make sure it doesn't get too mushy. Know what it is you're doing and stick to it, for a few minutes at least, before you shift your focus.

It also helps to practise any individual meditation once a day for four consecutive days. This is what takes you beyond the initial awkwardness and engraves the practice in long-term memory. Otherwise walking meditations will be little more than a nice idea that you dabble with occasionally.

Walking meditations

MEDITATION ONE: WALKING COMFORTABLY

An old Buddhist aphorism goes, 'when walking, just walk.' In other words, focus on the sensations of the body moving.

If we are anxious, we walk anxiously. You can see it in any city street. People walk with a stiff posture, hunched shoulders, tight breathing and blank eyes. Their anxieties are mirrored in their gait.

If you pay attention to how you are walking, you'll soon be walking more comfortably. In this meditation, you aim to walk with no excess tension. The body should feel balanced and open. The hips and shoulders swing easily. The breathing may synchronise with the footsteps. It can help to scan the body up and down as you walk, allowing the movement to free up tensions. You could say a mantra or an affirmation in time with your steps, if you wish.

When walking you'll still be subject to distractions. The usual principles apply: focus on your object (in this case, the body), and watch other thoughts and sensations with detachment. When you find you've 'jumped the fence', then tick off the distraction and return to the body.

MEDITATION TWO: COUNTING THE STEPS

If you've burst out of the office at the end of the day with your mind in chaos, you'll need a very crude and obvious meditation object to focus on, or you'll lose it. In this case, you count your footsteps. This meditation seems rather silly but it is an excellent emergency measure.

Since we can all count automatically, we need to make the counting more complex to stay with it. You walk at your usual pace but first count from one to five steps, then one to six steps, then one to seven and one to eight. Then back to one to five. So the meditation goes "1,2,3,4,5! 1,2,3,4,5,6! 1,2,3,4,5,6,7! 1,2,3,4,5,6,7,8!" And so on.

You have to pay attention to do this, or you'll soon find you're up to 15. Within a minute or two, you find you've stopped thinking about work and you realise, "It's quite a nice day out here!"

MEDITATION THREE: THE BREATH

In this meditation, you synchronise your breathing and footsteps, the way runners often do. You find out roughly how many steps you take as you breathe in, and roughly how many steps you take as you breathe out, and set that up as a pattern. Usually the out-breath is a little longer than the in-breath.

Mentally you count the steps. You may count three steps as you breathe in and four as you breathe out. Or you may have a two-three rhythm or a five-five rhythm. Just do what feels natural. And if the rhythm changes as you continue to walk, then change the count.

As a variant, you could just attempt to breath deeply and regularly for a few minutes as you walk. Your focus here will be on the mechanics of breathing itself. It's quite likely that the breath will fit into the rhythm of the steps anyway.

I usually don't recommend you breathe deeply when you meditate, but this is an exception. We all lose lung capacity steadily as we age. Elderly people barely breathe at all. Five minutes a day opening the lungs fully as we walk would be good for all of us.

MEDITATION FOUR: RANDOM SOUNDS

The three practices above all focus you inwards on your body and the breath. Nonetheless, by extracting you from thoughts they'll automatically enhance your awareness of your surroundings. It's always good to get grounded in the body first, but you can also meditate on external things such as sounds, sights, smells or all of these at once.

If you are meditating on sounds, the art is to highlight or hold on to each one for several seconds at least. This is what slows the mind down. If you skim too quickly from sensation to sensation, you'll soon skim back into thought. You actively focus on sounds and linger with each one, while passively noticing the other sensations. It's not that the other sensations are bad, or distractions that have to be avoided. It's just that deeper focus slows the mind down and is more satisfying.

MEDITATION FIVE: VISUAL OBJECTS

When we walk, there are hundreds of visual objects that can catch our eyes. As with sounds, the meditation won't work if you let the mind skim too rapidly. You'll fail to make genuine contact with any one of them. In other words, you won't really bring them into focus.

Therefore, as you walk, let your eyes move as they wish from tree to sky to grass to footpath, but do it slowly. Linger with each one for at least 10-15 seconds. Don't go looking for something new. Wait with one thing till something else grabs you. It's even better if you return to the body or the breath between each object. This will keep you grounded. You could also do the 'Snapshot' meditation from the last chapter.

MEDITATION SIX: WIND

This ancient practice is quite delicious. You focus on the movement of air over your body, as you walk or even sit outside. Even on a still day, the air masses shift around you, touching your cheek, neck or leg in succession. This is a very sensual practice. It feels like the earth is breathing over you. It's quite passive, like listening to sounds. You just wait for the next lick of air on your skin.

MEDITATION SEVEN: BEING PRESENT

In this practice, you focus on whatever sensation catches your attention in the moment. What makes this different from a stroll in the park is that you linger with each one for at least 10 seconds until something else replaces it. You sink into the detail: the smell of the earth, the sight of birds fighting, a blast of wind in your ear, the crunch of gravel underfoot. It's still a discipline. You notice when you're lost and return to the present.

Chapter nineteen

Being Present and Aware

It seems obvious to most people that you have to sit down to meditate. In fact, this is just the first stage, and it's unfortunate that many experienced meditators never go beyond it. They get stuck at square one.

The ideal is to integrate those tranquil inner spaces into your day. This is just as much of a discipline as sitting meditation. Once you've found that deep calm and clarity, you shouldn't lose it completely when you get up off your chair.

Trainee monks in Thailand do a lot of sitting meditation, but when they become an abbot, with all the responsibilities that implies, they do very little. It's assumed they can hold that relaxed and alert quality of mind in everything they do. That's one sign of their accomplishment.

A Zen master was asked, "How often do you meditate?" He answered, "When am I not meditating?" Obviously he understood the question differently from the questioner. Even a master has to eat, go to the toilet, and deal with difficult people. He still gets angry and sad from time to time, sickens and dies. Can he 'meditate' through all of that ?

To be honest, he probably can't; but the ideal is worth striving for. We can at least try to be centred and aware all day long. Sitting meditation can be a temporary escape from living, but it's not an ultimate solution. Life has a habit of muscling its way in. Meditation doesn't magically dispel the turbulence of living. It just enables you to find the point of balance.

A meditator doesn't calm the waves. He or she just floats like a cork on the ups and downs. The best way to stay afloat is to monitor what's happening in the moment. In other words, you know what you're doing as you're doing it, and you can chose your responses, even in the worst situations.

This may sound obvious, but this kind of moment-to-moment awareness goes against the grain of our habits. We tend to operate on automatic pilot. We can shuffle or zoom through the day not sensing or feeling anything clearly. What is worse, we can be too distracted to realise it. Some days, we're just not here at all.

Operating on automatic pilot does give the mind a break. It is restful, but it blurs our perception of reality and so is a mixed blessing. Just because we wake up in the morning doesn't mean we are fully here.

Many of us choose to be more or less unaware. We switch on the TV and read the paper and have a drink and move from one distraction to another all day. Often it takes an illness like cancer to make people wake up. Such people often say they now see what is important - feeling the dawn air, walking around the garden, a moment with a friend. Being awake, in other words.

The Buddha said, "When walking, just walk. When eating, just eat. Similarly when standing, sitting, getting dressed or going to the toilet." Our problem is that when walking, we think about work. At work, we think about sex. When with our lover or spouse we think about last night's TV. When watching TV, we also eat, read the newspaper and talk to someone. It is not surprising that the mind gets confused and exhausted. And we don't enjoy the TV or the food, or making love as much as we could.

THE SYSTEMATIC DEVELOPMENT OF AWARENESS

Being present and aware during the day doesn't come automatically. You need to practise it, starting with activities that are relatively simple or pleasant.

First we find we can remain relaxed and alert with our eyes open.

Then while walking in the park or on the beach. Then while doing simple activities such as preparing a meal or having a shower.

The original Buddhist instructions spelled it all out, step by step, for the wandering holy men of that time. First, you would meditate with eyes closed, sitting under a tree. Then you keep that quality of mind with your eyes open. Then you practise walking to and fro in front of your tree, realising that you don't have to be distracted by what you see.

Then you walk mindfully to the local village to scrounge some food. There are many more temptations here. The hustle and bustle can be quite attractive after a long morning's meditation. A beautiful young woman puts food in your bowl and reminds you what you are missing. Even the very simple life of a begging monk can be full of mental turmoil.

Then you walk back to your tree, doing your walking meditation. Then the eating meditation. Then the lying down and trying not to fall asleep meditation. Then you get up mindfully and rearrange your clothing. You walk to one side and urinate, mindfully hearing your urine fall on the dry forest leaves. These can all be conscious meditations, with clear beginnings and endings.

Throughout the day, you also would observe your natural surroundings. You could formally or informally meditate on earth, water, fire, light and space. Or simply notice how weather and light and nature change around you during the 24-hour cycle. You would also observe the cycles of sensation, thought and mood within your mind and body during the day. Though few of us can do this systematically, the benefits of this kind of practice are incalculable.

MAKING SIMPLE ACTIVITIES INTO MEDITATIONS

Because being present seems like a good idea, you may resolve that, "Today I am going to live in the present!" However, it is better to be more modest with your goals. Don't try to be present for an hour or a day. Just try for a few seconds or minutes at a time. Aim for high quality and short duration.

It can be surprisingly satisfying. Try to eat a biscuit consciously. Enjoy watering your plants. Brush your teeth deliberately. Hang out the washing as if it was important to do it well.

I often do the 'kitchen sink' meditations while preparing food. Sometimes I focus on one sense, such as sound. I listen to each sound I make: cutting the apple, putting the knife down, the squeal of the tap and the water running, the bowl scraping on the bench, a foot shuffle, the fridge door opening, the clang as I place something on a rack, and so on.

I hold my mind to the task by saying the word 'sound' silently, each time I breathe out. I am aware of other sensations of course, but I highlight the sounds.

Alternatively, I notice input from any sense. The texture of the knife, fruit, water, the door handle. The glistening skin of a capsicum, patterns of light and shadow, a stain on the bench. Or the sensations in my arm as I lift something.

I non-verbally ask myself, "Where is my mind, right now?" It is amazing how rapidly my mind can disappear into thought. And how interesting the sense world can be if we focus on it.

The Japanese tea ceremony is a similar multi-sensory meditation. As the guest, you watch each movement of the tea-maker. You enjoy the decorations in the room, hear the sounds, watch the steam, feel and look at the bowl, taste the tea and feel yourself swallowing. You become tranquil by focusing on one small detail after another.

I do the same when I'm at a cafe. If the conversation around me seems pointless, I tune out discreetly for a few seconds. I deliberately taste my coffee. Quite slowly, I reach out my hand, feel it make contact with the cup and then feel the muscles tense to raise it and bring it to my lips. I consciously smell the aroma, tilt the cup, feel the froth and the liquid coming through my lips and feel my taste buds respond.

I let this experience play through my mind, and then deliberately put down the coffee, noticing the very moment my hand separates from the cup. And I relish the mental space this mindful activity has given me.

Similarly, I will focus on the sensations of having a shower: the smell of soap, the sounds and texture of water, the warmth and skin response, the pleasurable bodily movements . . .

Moving from my car to the supermarket is another typical meditation for me. I hear the engine die away as I switch off the ignition. I take a deep breath or two and let my body settle. I consciously reach for the door handle, feeling the texture and resistance as I open it. I notice the surprisingly complex body movements that go with getting up from the seat. And finally, I take in the trees and the sky as I walk across the carpark. It takes some effort to maintain unbroken focus on these simple activities.

Being Present

This meditation lets you move serially from one sensory object to another as they come to mind. Or you could multi-layer your meditation by focusing primarily on the breath and adding in new things as they arise. It's quite okay to move your point of focus, so long as you stay with each one for at least ten seconds.

INSTRUCTIONS

1.   Sit down and relax the body and breathing as usual.
     Notice the strongest sensation and focus on it.
     It could be the breath, or a shoulder pain, or a lawn mower outside. Let your mind sink into it. Explore the detail.

2.   Don't hold the object tightly. If something else catches your attention - a passing car, an itch - shift your focus to that. Hold that sensation until something else calls you.

3.   Let your mind shift from sensation to sensation.
     Hold each one for at least 10 seconds.
     Or go deeply into any one.
     Check yourself occasionally: Ask, "Am I in the present?" or, "Where is the mind right now?"

Chapter twenty

The Deeper States

We have all seen advertising images of the perfect meditator. In the clear light of morning, she sits almost naked on a beach, the sunlight illuminating her perfect yoga body. Her thoughts, if she has any, are obviously blissful and radiant.

She seems a universe away from you, as you sit in your untidy bedroom, tired and irritated after a day at work. "I'll never be able to meditate!", you think, as you succumb to one aggravating thought after another.

We usually meditate with some awareness of peripheral thoughts and sensations, but occasionally we drop beyond all that. We taste something special and unique, and think, "That's what that yogi on the beach feels! This is it!"

These beautiful states usually occur at the edge of sleep. This is when our metabolism slows down, the body becomes perfectly still and the last thoughts dissolve into space. It is usually the moment before oblivion.

This sleep threshold state is exquisite, but difficult to hold. Usually when the body goes to sleep, the mind follows. By losing consciousness, we stumble at the threshold and miss the deeper states of mind. A good meditator, however, can stay alert as she enters the dream state. She doesn't stumble.

GOING INTO THETA

The sleep threshold is technically called 'stage one sleep'. This is the first of four sleep stages, each of which has its own signature brain wave pattern. Stage one sleep is when the slow 'theta' brain waves start emerging from the alpha waves of the waking mind.

This state is also called 'paradoxical sleep', because it's not quite sleep or wakefulness. In fact, it's often an oscillation between the two. One part of you wants to collapse into sleep and the other part is trying to remain awake, and you wobble between them. If you're battling to stay awake in a boring meeting, for example, you're going into stage one sleep. On an electroencephalograph, you can even see the struggle between the alpha and theta waves.

Usually, we're only semi-conscious in theta. But sometimes, we're more alert than usual and this is when it gets beautiful. This can also happen when you're waking from a light afternoon nap. For a few seconds there are no thoughts at all. The mind feels delicate and fresh. You are only just conscious and it feels lovely!

You may notice this theta state occasionally as you fall asleep at night. As you relax, you let thoughts go and shift into sensing mode. You feel the sheets against your skin and the body feels softer as the muscle tension subsides.

As you relax more, you seem to disconnect from your body. You may know you're still awake, but not know if you're lying on your left or right side. You no longer know whether you're touching your partner or not. Your body is disappearing, bit by bit, as you surrender to the depths.

Yet you can still be conscious. You haven't died. You still feel the subtle vibrations of life within you - spacious, tingling and warm, like the humming of the cells - which seem to be everywhere and nowhere. It has a mood also, which is something like, "God, this is lovely!" Then you fall asleep and lose it.

People often enter this 'body asleep, mind awake' state when I guide meditations in class. Afterwards they may say, "I seemed to be asleep but I know I was awake. I heard every word you said." Or they say, "I could hear you talking but you seemed very far away".

I teach many beginners and as they relax, they naturally start to fall asleep. Each time I speak in a guided meditation, it wakes them up again. So they fall asleep and then pull back again, many times.

Eventually the oscillations become small and controllable and the meditator can balance on the edge. As one woman said, "I must have fallen asleep (and woken up) about fifty times."

This ability distinguishes a good meditator from someone who just relaxes when he 'meditates'. Back in the alpha zone as we start to relax, we have a choice of two paths. We can follow decades of habit and subside towards sleep. We may not quite fall off the chair, but our 'meditation' can be rather torpid.

Alternatively, we can stay awake as the body goes to sleep. This gives us the best of both worlds. It is not an either/or choice. This way you get even deeper relaxation and mental clarity. When you can hold this state, it becomes serene, clear and timeless. You have entered the palace of the gods.

Part of the beauty of this state is that thoughts have virtually disappeared. People often ask me in frustration, "How can I block my thoughts? They're driving me crazy!" There are only three good ways that I know of.

The first is to become intently absorbed in something sensual. The second is to disengage from thoughts the moment they arise, by 'just watching' them. The third is to keep the mind awake as the body goes to sleep.

LETTING GO THE SELF

Usually we are either awake, and therefore aware of self, or asleep and unconscious of self. There's a third possibility however. On the sleep threshold you can forget yourself (as you do when you fall asleep) but still retain consciousness. There is awareness but little awareness of self. For this reason, the sleep threshold is the first of what are called the 'transpersonal' states.

If this seems rather mystical, let me explain it this way. The daily cycle from sleep to wakefulness and back again is also a cycle from self to non-self. When awake we have a strong sense of who we are and when asleep, almost none.

Anxiety magnifies the sense of self even further. People who are extremely anxious or depressed assess every sensation or experience in terms of, "Is this good or bad for Me?" Their thoughts compulsively revolve around their problems, and they barely notice the world beyond. Their universe rotates around 'I'.

A person who is psychologically healthy, or just more relaxed, is less preoccupied with self. He or she can enjoy things that don't directly relate to personal well-being - music, another person, the beauty of an autumn day. He also sees his problems with more detachment.

Thinking is driven by our habitual fears, anger and desire. Just to be awake always involves some anxiety, since we are always looking out for Number One. We can't fall asleep unless we let go that orientation to self. The 'body asleep, mind awake' state occurs when we abandon that emotional drive.

This is a colossal relief. If you remain awake, there is just pure awareness, with no agenda. Both the self-oriented thoughts and the sense of self have gone. The feeling is best described as a delicate ecstasy. It is 'ec-static' in its literal meaning of 'standing outside' oneself.

At the sleep threshold, the sense of self dissolves enormously. It is like 'a little death' - a term the Elizabethan poets used to describe orgasm. It is beautiful to forget yourself so utterly and yet be awake enough to enjoy it. A good meditator, like a good lover, can protract this pleasure rather than letting it vanish in an instant.

Of course, sleep also makes you oblivious to self, but in sleep, the thoughts just go underground and continue to stir you up. If you stay alert on the threshold however, new thoughts dissolve instantly. When the mind is still, the body becomes still and your metabolic rate may drop to its lowest point within minutes. Normal sleep, with its underlying turbulence, might take hours to reach this state. This is why meditation, minute for minute, relaxes the body more deeply than sleep.

As the body relaxes, it releases pent-up energy. Many people use meditation like a health-food bar to give them a boost during the day. Alternatively, we can reinvest the energy into the meditation. If we do, we develop a tranquil mind with crystal clarity and split-second awareness.

Since most of us are somewhat sleep-deprived, we have a strong compulsion to fall asleep whenever we can. I find it hard to convince people that it is better to stay alert. That seems like quite a sacrifice for something they can't imagine. I find that people can't take my word for it. They have to repeatedly taste this state before they realise its value. It usually takes several weeks of classes before they choose to be awake rather than semi-conscious when they relax.

HYPNAGOGIA

When you first go into theta you tend to oscillate between wakefulness and sleep. Particularly if you are tired, you will bob in and out a lot. You may suddenly 'wake up' and think, "where was I the last few seconds?"

As you get more stable, the body gets very still and this feels marvellous. The mental quality however can still be rather vague. I personally feel this state as being like a soft mist in moonlight, or like moonstone or white opal.

You can remain here if you wish, or you could let the mind wake up and explore its surroundings. This doesn't break the tranquility. In fact, it enhances your awareness of it. It also opens up new worlds.

In particular, you may notice what is called 'hypnagogic' imagery. These first appear as rapid and very strange dream images - an ambulance roosting in a tree, a dog discussing mathematics, for example. These differ from 'normal' dreams in several ways.

They tend to be extremely quick. You can get dozens of images in a second. They're often more bizarre than normal dreams. Even less than in dreams, they lack an ego-reference, or an 'I' that watches them. They often come as sonic or tactile hallucinations, and may contain fragments of intense thought. Despite their complexity, they're usually quite subtle and hard to follow. You can easily miss them.

It is like watching the vast complexity of the brain at work. It is quite possible that this is exactly what it is. Do these images represent the thousands of neural exchanges in the brain each second?

When people first notice these little dreams, it shocks them back into wakefulness. They know it's a sign they've lost control and they've certainly lost their meditation object. But with skill and practice, you can become stable in this dream state. In other words, with only a residual sense of yourself and your body, you can stay in control. Like Ulysses strapped to the mast, you can enjoy the song of the sirens without becoming their victim.

The hypnagogic state is worth exploring for its enchantment value alone. However, as you become more stable here, its quality changes too. The imagery becomes more coherent and profound. Brilliant insights can arise. Poetry, music, lateral thoughts, extraordinary perspectives on reality can spring up, without any ego-involvement on your part.

In fact, anything the human mind has ever been capable of can arise in this state. It is the source of all inspiration. You know what the old Indian sages mean when they talk about 'the play of consciousness' because you can see it happening in yourself.

FOUR STATES OF CONSCIOUSNESS

Useful as the hypnagogic state is, there are still deeper states of mind. In the East, there are considered to be four classical stages of 'awakening', or the full development of consciousness. These are:

1.   being awake while awake
2.   being awake while dreaming
3.   being awake in dreamless sleep, and
4.   integrating all three states at once.

The first state, being awake while awake, means to be fully aware of thoughts, sensations and feelings as they arise. It is the opposite of running on automatic pilot or day-dreaming or sleep-walking through life. It is a continuous self-reflective awareness in the beta and alpha states of waking life.

The second state is to be awake in theta, as I describe it above. The third state is to be awake in dreamless sleep, when the brain emits the very slow delta brain waves. Only the very best meditators can stay conscious in this state. These are the profound depths of trance where there can be consciousness, but no 'you' at all.

It is a state of unimaginable peace and delight. It is described as being one with God or the cosmos. The Tibetans call it 'the pregnant void', or the emptiness from which all things arise. Mystics describe it as the the end of the journey. What else could you possibly want?

Its major shortcoming is that it doesn't last. You still have to come back to your toothache and sore back, and earn your daily bread. So the ideal state, the fourth, is to integrate all three states at once, like living in three mutually contradictory realities.

This is to embody the bliss of deep trance while arguing with your three-year-old over breakfast. In the deep state, you could watch the destruction of galaxies with equanimity, but in daily life it is important to also have matching socks. If you can integrate all three states, you still go and look for the missing sock.

HOW DO YOU GO INTO THETA?

We go into theta any time we're sleepy. The real question is, how do you consciously enter theta and stay there? The simple answer is that you do what you always do: you focus on one thing and watch other thoughts and sensations with detachment. However, you do this very much better than usual.

Meditation is a very forgiving practice. Often we don't focus very well and the mind gets tangled in thoughts. Nonetheless we still relax and the mind feels more settled afterwards. However you need to do better than this to stay conscious in theta.

As you relax, the way you perceive the meditation object changes in stages we could describe as: unfocused, focusing with struggle, focusing without struggle, and absorption. At first, your focus is scattered. You can't stay with the object more than a second or two. This is the 'unfocused' stage.

As you start relaxing, you can focus better, but it's still a struggle. As you settle in, however, it's much easier to hold the object, and the surrounding thoughts and sensations don't bother you. You're now 'focusing without struggle'.

You now go deeper into the object. If you explore it with a kind of lazy curiosity, you may find the background thoughts and sensations vanish altogether for seconds at a time. This is called a state of 'absorption', or 'samadhi', where there is nothing in the mind but the object. You merge into it.

This is the point at which you usually drop into theta. The background thoughts have been eclipsed. By focusing totally on an object, you've forgotten yourself. Time can slow right down and almost stop.

At this point, you often lose the object, drop into moments of unconsciousness or get distracted by hypnagogic imagery. To stay in control, you have to develop acute moment-to-moment focus. You also need excellent awareness, so you can notice the imagery without falling in love with it.

Personally, I check myself the whole way down. Typically, I will focus on the breath to start with and ask, 'did I catch the exact moment that breath stopped?' If my mind is a little turbulent, I can't really be sure.

As my mind settles, I switch to the heartbeat and ask, "Did I catch the very beginning of that beat?" When I'm sharp enough to do that, I then go into the gap between the beats and ask, "What's happening here?"

Interestingly, this is not a dead or empty space. There is a delicate play of almost invisible sensation here, which has a rhythmic ebb and flow like all living processes. When I'm focused enough to notice the rise and fall of these subtle sensations, I'm likely to be going into theta. In other words, I sharpen my focus like increasing the magnification on a microscope. I go deeper into the detail of my object, whenever I can.

It's rare to settle into high-detail focus for more than a few seconds without also noticing peripheral things with equal clarity. You'll find that absorption and the deeper states do not need to obliterate your awareness of everything else.

Furthermore, you can't force yourself to focus if your mind is turbulent. Until you've acknowledged what's troubling you, it usually won't let you go. Good focus comes not by holding tight to the object but by completely letting go everything else. You usually have to straighten out the many imbalances before finding absolute balance. This takes time and acceptance and there aren't any short cuts.

GOOD AWARENESS

A parallel way to enter theta is to be hyper-aware. In other words, if you notice the changing landscape as you relax, you can focus on it to take you deeper. If you tune into the physical and mental signs, they act as biofeedback mechanisms and accelerate the process.

The physical signs that you are entering theta are: the body feeling numb, floating, hollow or vanishing; a great stillness and the breathing almost stopped; very faint sensations of 'energy-flow' in your vanishing body.

The mental signs are: moments of oblivion or a sense of emptiness; hypnagogic imagery or irrational thoughts; a sense of extreme detachment or dissociation and an absence of self; timelessness, and an impersonal happiness or bliss.

To stay in this stage, you need to notice these signs with almost complete indifference. If you get excited and say, "what was that?", you're bound to lose it and drift back into alpha.

When you are capable of saying 'no' to absolutely everything, you are then free to say 'yes'. You can pluck an image or mood or insight from the stream of consciousness, and explore it. Ideally you are quiet and very dispassionate as you do it. You can lose your clear, mirror-like mind in a flash unless you're vigilant.

Inner Space

This is actually a meditation within a meditation. Five or ten minutes into a sitting when you feel relaxed and lucid, you can consciously go deeper. You do it by increasing the magnification on your microscope. In the example below I've focused on the body, but you can do it with any meditation object. I should add that this exercise won't work unless you've already allowed the background disturbances to clear.

INSTRUCTIONS

1.   Try to catch the micro-second the breath stops.
     Also notice exactly where and when it seems to start.
     Don't hurry the new breath. Let it come when it wants to.
     Sink into the space between out-breath and in-breath.

2.   In that space, feel the heartbeat.
     Try to catch the exact start and finish of the heartbeat.
     Now sink into the space between the beats.
     Notice the background hum of sensation there.

3.   Notice how those sensations also rise and fall.
     Try to catch the moment they come and go.
     Go into the background space between the sensations.

4.   Notice how still the mind and body have become.
     What else is occurring in the periphery of consciousness?
     Enjoy the clarity and moment-to-moment alertness.
     Go deeper by exploring anything in microscopic detail.

Chapter twenty-one

Visualisation

For some people, visualisation *is* meditation. It's how and why they meditate. They sit down and start actively fantasising as a way of thinking in pictures. They may contemplate an inspiring idea in order to heal themselves, or to change negative thought patterns, or to contact the spiritual world or to imagine their future.

They usually place a high premium on getting inspiration when they sit. The Western tradition, from the medieval Catholic Church to the New Age gurus, gives them a lot of encouragement to do this. This is a very Western way of meditating.

The Eastern practices, on the other hand, emphasise tranquility and mental clarity. Visualisation, when used at all, tends to be quite simple, on the principle that simple things take you deeper than complex ones. Tranquility, not thought, is seen as the prerequisite for wisdom.

It's not that one approach is better than the other. It's just that East and West have differing goals and methods. Even their spirituality is different. The Western mystics such as St Francis and St Theresa tend towards tearful ecstasies. In the East, you find the serene calm of the Buddha.

The Western approach is more muscular and active. The great exemplar of this is St Ignatius, the founder of the Jesuit order, who was a soldier, after all. His 'Spiritual Exercises' ask you to evoke images to make yourself a better Christian. For example, you could imagine being in Nazareth talking to Jesus and taking advice from him. St Ignatius regarded meditation as 'an exercise of the will' to enhance the good and repress your bad instincts.

His descendants, the American thought-control schools, train people to imagine themselves confident and positive and achieving their goals, while suppressing 'negative' thoughts. This may seem to be non-religious, but it usually contains certain implicit beliefs that are rarely questioned. A common assumption is that thoughts have an almost magical effect and need to be controlled. In other words, what you think or believe, good or bad, will come true.

Personally, I doubt this. I recently received a panicky call from a woman with cancer. "I've got to stop every negative thought", she said. "How can I do it?" Any meditator could tell her that we can't dominate our thoughts this way. They have a will of their own.

KNOW WHAT YOU'RE TRYING TO DO

The Western approach has much of value in it but my own tendencies lean to the East. I've described the Western approach above so you don't get confused between the two. It's important to know what you're trying to do. Are you using an image to relax and deepen a mood, or as a prop for contemplative thought? These are quite different purposes. You can mix them, but they often fit awkwardly together.

Meditation usually works because it is so simple. However people often visualise for quite complicated purposes. The effort involved can work against the desire for a calm, clear mind. People who love visualisation tend to neglect the need to relax properly. They commonly focus on the breath or the body for just a minute or two, before leaping into their visualisations. In their enthusiasm for inspiration, they can forget the spade work that keeps the wellspring open.

Most meditations are clear and logical practices. Visualising, however, is very idiosyncratic. There is no one way to do it. Just as some people never seem to dream and some dream all night, the way people work with their imagination is as personal as can be.

Furthermore, visualising is rarely a 'pure' practice. Meditation, as I explain it in this book, is designed to simplify and clear the mind - a return to the essence of consciousness. Visualisation, however, naturally blends with thinking, with imaginative invention, with self-analysis and with religious and philosophic beliefs. It's a kind of pure meditation *plus* whatever you like.

This doesn't have to be a jumble. If you relax into the theta state, and lay a foundation of physical calm and mental clarity, your imagery can be strong and natural. It will draw from the depths of the unconscious and can really become a dialogue with the hidden powers of the mind.

WORKING WITH A SINGLE IMAGE

Visualisation is a technique that only suits about one person in four. These are the people who naturally think in images. It can be taught, but basically it's a genetic endowment, like blue or brown eyes. You either have it or you don't. It is possible to learn it, but it may not be worth the bother. There are many other ways to meditate.

But if you would like to use imagery more, you can cultivate it. You can use an image just like any meditation object: you focus on it and when the mind wanders off, you return to it. Using an image or a visualisation in this way can work just as well as the breath or a mantra.

Usually the simplest images take you deepest. You may get bored with the breath, but you can easily imagine the ocean, an apple, the night sky, your backyard, your cat or a favourite painting, or even play a tune over in your head. In fact, focusing on something imaginary may work better for you than something 'real'.

Some people are strongly visual, but many more of us have a 'kinesthetic' imagination. We 'see' things as much via feeling or mood and can as easily evoke sound, touch, smell or taste. You can imagine a friend's dog, for example - the long fur, the snuffly mouth in your ear, the romping energy and the doggy smell - without the visuals being particularly clear.

Read the following sequence slowly. Give each image and its associated mood a few seconds to arise. Notice which of the senses is strongest. Notice if your body relaxes into, or recoils from, individual images. Linger on those that grab you. I am sure some will catch your attention more than others:

*   stroking a cat
*   chronic pain
*   kissing someone you love
*   the sound of an open fire
*   cold morning air
*   a familiar tool
*   water
*   peeling an orange
*   sipping coffee
*   chopping wood

Which was strongest, and which precise detail of those images caught your attention the most? Those that worked best probably evoked more than one sense and an emotional tone as well. In other words, you responded as if you were actually there.

If you imagine being under a cold shower, your skin should literally contract. If you then imagine basking in the sun, you feel it expanding. If you are meditating for healing, for example, this body response is much more important than clear visuals.

GUIDED VISUALISATIONS

People commonly encounter visualisations as a guided meditation on a tape or in a class. Typically, you lie on the floor and are talked through a storyline sequence of images. These can be very pleasant, like going to an interactive movie, and for children they are ideal. There is little effort or skill required on your part because someone else is leading you.

These visualisations usually contain similar ingredients, each of which tends to be a good metaphor of meditation itself. For example, you imagine yourself being alone. In other words, you let go your involvement with others and come back to yourself. This is your first taste of solitude.

Then you imagine descending a staircase. In other words, you go deep inside yourself, step by step, away from the outer world. At the bottom, you then walk into an attractive landscape. This shifts you into a beautiful present, rich in sensual images.

These visualisations often use questions to awaken your imagination. You go into a garden and what do you see? You open a box and what is there? You see a wise man and what do you ask him? The results can be illuminating.

Before you finish, it's useful to choose a single image from the scene to remind you of it. This can act as a talisman later. You can recall the image and it will partly reawaken the feeling of the meditation.

In fact, places are surprisingly easy to imagine. Your living room, the walk to work, a friend's house, a familiar park or beach would all work well. You could just imagine the view from your window. One of my students was a depressed real estate salesman. The only way he could meditate at all was to go through every house he had ever sold.

You could also evoke imaginary places to match your mood. Go to the most perfect health spa you can imagine. Go to Heaven and talk to the angels. Imagine a place that would feel like your true home. Go to ancient Greece or Celtic Ireland or pre-European Polynesia. And see yourself doing what you want to do there.

FINDING THE IMAGE STREAM

I was not a natural visualiser, so it may interest you to know how I learnt to do it. In my initial training I was encouraged to focus purely on physical sensation. I was taught to ignore images as being distractions and 'not real'.

When I took up the Tibetan practices, however, all that changed. My training involved literally tens of thousands of prostrations, mantra and accompanying visualisations. This was not at all what I thought of as meditation.

Even worse, after years of ignoring images, I now found myself apparently unable to visualise at all. I sympathise completely with students who say, "I can't see anything when I try to visualise!" I was trying to visualise deities, colours, trees, crystal palaces, animals, jewels, energy flows in the body, and I was getting nothing at all.

Yet I doggedly persisted and quite suddenly, early one morning, it happened. It was like a door flying open. The imagery had always been there. I just hadn't looked in the right direction. The images didn't compete with or replace reality. They were like a superimposition, or double image, overlaying it. They were subtle, but also quite rich and convincing. They weren't particularly vivid and bright like images on a picture screen, but they were definitely there.

Once I knew how to look, the image bank opened. Memories arose in extraordinary detail from my childhood and youth. With this vast picture library available to me, I now found visualising an easy practice.

For one whole month, I mentally returned for a few minutes each day to my childhood home to see what else I could remember. I never got to the end of it. A few years later, I was even able to check if the details were correct. The house was rented out to students by this time and they were quite happy to let me go right through it. I found that I wasn't far wrong in my memories.

Now, when I meditate, I often have a quiet trickle of images from every sense in the background. Occasionally, it erupts into a cacophony like a Hollywood blockbuster. At other times it will almost vanish. It seems that some part of my mind is always dreaming, day and night, even as I eat breakfast, answer the telephone and work on the computer.

We don't notice this continual stream of images because our minds are too busy with thoughts. These images are like the stars that we can't see when the sun is out. We only notice them when dreaming or at the edge of sleep.

Over the years, the quality of the images has changed. The parade of images from youth, childhood and infancy has largely finished. They now seem to arise from a place beyond my personal history. They may come from what the psychologist Jung would call 'the collective unconscious'. Much of it, I am sure, is due to 'cryptomnesia' - the ability of the mind to invent strong images from sources in long-forgotten books and movies.

ADD-ON IMAGERY

Because of my training, I am always aware of my body, regardless of the kind of meditation I do. So I tend to use imagery as an add-on to a breath or bodyscan meditation.

For example, it's easy to imagine the breath as a wave, ebbing and flowing in the body. Or imagine it massaging you from the inside. Or see it as a swing, or a circular motion, or a rocking cradle. These images aren't distractions. They can increase your focus.

When you scan the body, you could imagine white light, or spring water, or good energy flowing through it. You could send the vibration of a mantra or affirmation to parts that require it. You could gradually fill the body with blue or gold light. Or you could imagine the seven colours of the spectrum radiating from the centres of the seven regions. More on this in chapter 22.

It's common for images and memories to occasionally pop up in the mind when we sit. This happens naturally as we relax. The words fade away and pictures arise. It's very easy to weave them into the fabric of your meditation.

You can use an image or memory as a temporary point of focus, just as you could with a sound or a pain. When an image arises, don't get excited and ask, "What does this mean?" Just examine it dispassionately, noting its sensual qualities of colour, shape and texture, just as you would with a flower or a candle in front of you. Let the image go when it fades and return to your original focus.

DEVELOPING THE SKILLS

Most people have difficulty visualising because they never consciously look at anything. When did you last examine a rose in detail? An artist or an interior designer, on the other hand, would have no trouble imagining a precise colour, simply because she's trained herself to do so.

So it's good to go back to basics. If you want to imagine colour, then focus on a particular colour for several days till you really become familiar with it. To focus on 'yellow' for example, you could consciously notice all the yellow things you see during the day. You'll then find it easier to imagine the colour when you meditate later. Or focus on something yellow as in the 'Visual Object' meditation in Chapter 17.

Colours are usually easier to imagine if linked with an object. You could go through the spectrum imagining in turn a red tomato, an orange orange, a yellow daffodil, a green leaf, the blue of the sky and so on.

In the East, you were also trained to imagine earth, water, fire and air, in all their permutations, the objects of the five senses, and the place and texture of all the organs, muscles and bones in your body.

All this was done in great detail. To meditate on yellow, for example, you would collect yellow flowers and arrange them in a bowl before you. You would gaze at them while saying the word 'yellow', slowly imprinting the colour in consciousness.

After a day or two, you would be able to see the colour with your eyes closed, and even while walking around, doing ordinary activities. When you became totally immersed in the colour, they said, the whole world would occasionally turn yellow. You would really know what yellow is and what it does to you. So then you move on to red.

HEALING MEDITATIONS

The most useful thing you can do when you're sick is to relax deeply when you can, and to stay out of the stress zone during the day. This is because all the systems in the body, and especially the immune system, work best when we're relaxed. This puts no undue pressure on the body, and gives it space to heal and restore itself. You don't need visualisation for this.

People often seek out meditation when they're sick, but with a different orientation. They feel that visualisations can help rally the troops and attack their illness. It will help them fight the enemy within. This can be useful, but it can also create strain. There are more sensitive ways to work. Let me describe some ways in which visualisations can help you if you're ill.

PURE AWARENESS

Awareness is probably the simplest and strongest practice of all. You simply focus on the site of your illness and allow all the physical and emotional sensations to arise. If you wish, you can imagine consciousness as a light that illuminates all the dark and hidden corners of the disease.

Ideally your attention should be curious and exploratory, like a child exploring the delicate structure of a living insect. A clear mind has no fear or anger or desire. It is non-judgemental and just sees what is there. Within a few seconds, you'll notice yourself relaxing, and the sensations and emotions changing, without your having to do anything at all.

It can be useful to find out what your illness looks like. Then, when you focus on it, you have some idea of the appearance of the organs and tissues, and the cells of the immune system. Use photographs and X-rays to enhance your awareness. These prompts can help you feel or 'see' in more detail than you would otherwise.

Awareness alone helps the healing process. I don't quite understand why, but it does. However, stop this kind of meditation if you find that it increases your anxiety. The bottom line is to relax in whatever way you can.

WASHING THE BODY WITH COLOUR

At the cellular level, healing really is a battle, but you don't have to see it this way. You can imagine washing the illness with light or love or nectar or a healing colour. Otherwise, imagine caressing or massaging the injured tissue in whatever way it wants.

You could ask your body, 'What colour do you want', and imagine that colour flowing through you. You could play music or say a mantra, and imagine the gentle vibrations of the sound harmonising the energies in your cells. Don't get too busy and try to make it all right. Just have a good time and let the body relax.

Health Spa

In this meditation, you imagine everything, real or fantastic, that would help you heal. Try not to be too busy with it. If a single detail calls, then go right into it. Visualisations act as holograms: any detail that catches your imagination will be as good as the whole picture.

INSTRUCTIONS

1. Check your body and breathing as usual.
   Feel the body loosening up.

2. Imagine the perfect place of healing for you:
   a health spa or crystal palace or temple in the mountains.
   Roam through it, enjoying the atmosphere.

3. Be as sensual as possible. Go for detail.
   Notice what you see and hear and eat and do.

   Feel the smooth edge and texture of a single leaf.
   Savour the song of this particular bird.

4. Now meet your team of healers.
   They could be real or imaginary people.
   The right doctor, a naturopath, a physiotherapist.
   Or they may include archetypal figures:
   a wise woman, herbalist, saint, Chinese sage.

5. Talk with them and decide what to do.
   They could even work on your body from inside.
   See yourself doing what would be good for you.

Chapter twenty-two

The Breath and Bodyscan Meditations revisited

Your body is always with you. Whatever practice you do, you're bound to have some awareness of your body as well. It's good to focus on in its own right, but it also interacts well with other practices. Your natural body awareness will tend to support and ground a visualisation or mantra, for example. It literally gives the experience more 'body'.

Meditations combine well. Since you can't avoid hearing sounds while focusing on the breath, then why not focus on both, alternating from one to the other? Similarly you can scan the body while saying an affirmation, or listen to sounds while doing your yoga or add a beautiful image while watching the breath.

To keep the instructions simple we say, 'focus on one object', but in fact several objects can work even better. You're not 'distracted' when you move from the breath to a candle to a sound. They're all sensual things that keep thoughts at bay, and help you to be in the present.

THE BREATH IS VERY VERSATILE

There are many ways of focusing on the breath itself, and of combining it with other practices. Let me give you an overview of the possibilities.

First, you could just focus on the breath 'as it is', without any additions. You can tune into the ever-changing sensations of the breath throughout the body and go into infinite depth. Since the breath is 'transparent', you also notice other sensations of life: the pulse, the common signs of relaxation, areas of pain etc.

You could count the breaths as described in Chapter 6. This anchors you and gives you more structure. Or use a mantra such as HAMSA, as described in Chapter 14. Or you could say an affirmation as you breathe, as described in Chapter 15.

Mantra are easy to combine with visualisations. So you could imagine the breath as a wave that ebbs and flows from the feet to the head, or imagine washing the body with sound. If you use a mantra like OM MANI PEME HUNG, you could imagine it reverberating through parts of your body.

You could also do a tactile visualisation. You could imagine 'breathing through' every place in the body in turn, from the scalp to your toes. You breathe through the aches and pains, and free them up. You could imagine that you are massaging your body with your mind (It is surprising how effective this is).

If you like to control the breath, you can imagine making it smoother and easier. You can place it down gently when you breathe out, and round off the turns. This can be quite luxurious.

You can do the breath meditation while walking or swimming, as described in Chapter 17. You could take four deep breaths while standing in a supermarket queue. You could 'breathe through' parts of your body when you do yoga or exercise or weights at the gym. And of course, the breath also combines easily with bodyscanning.

THE ADVANTAGES OF BODYSCANNING

When you scan, you have many options. You can scan quickly or slowly, up or down. You can do it plain, just noticing the bare sensations, or you could add visualisations or mantra. You don't have to scan right through. You may just explore certain areas of pain or pleasure. You can divide the body into seven regions or not, or just scan the centres of those regions.

Why all these options? First, we scan in order to focus the mind.

This is the bottom line. Secondly, scanning both feels, and is, profoundly good for our health. Thirdly, by scanning we enhance our self-awareness and know what it really feels like to be alive. Fourthly, we gain valuable insight into the interplay of body and mind.

Fifthly, scanning is like finding the instruction manual for the body we've got. Instead of blindly hoping it'll continue to work and do what we want it to do, we get to know it in intimate detail. Instead of sending orders from the head to the body, we can listen to the body's messages and co-operate much better with it.

USING A TEMPLATE

In Chapter 8, I suggested you divide the body into seven regions from top to bottom to give you a clear structure to work with. You can then spend 4, or 8, or 10 breaths in each place, depending on the pace you prefer.

This gives you a template, and a clear task to do. You may, for example, give yourself 10 breaths to fully explore the sensations in the chest before moving on. This kind of structure gives you more clarity and precision, and makes it easy to notice when you're distracted.

Yet neither scanning in distinct stages nor counting the breaths is essential. You could just stay in each place for as long as you like. You move on when it feels right, or you feel you've 'done it'. You don't even need to scan right through. It's quite enough to have the mind focused.

THE ENERGY-FIELD

We think of our bodies as being solid objects that are always much the same. When we scan, however, this isn't the body we focus on. We're actually tuning into the whole network of sensations within the body. We can call this 'the energy-field', and unlike our 'normal' body, this can change enormously.

For example, the body that walks into a restaurant looks much the same as the one that walks out. But if you've been eating and drinking too much, it could feel utterly different. By scanning, we focus on the body as we feel it rather than the body we see. Since these inner sensations are in continual flux and change markedly as we relax, we have a lot to focus on.

When we start a sitting, the mind typically notices what's wrong in the body. Scanning illuminates the body, and the mind is instinctively drawn to the tight and painful areas. Being aware of a tension is usually enough to start it releasing.

Furthermore, when you focus on an area, it tends to get warmer. Apparently, this temperature rise can even be measured. Focusing seems to temporarily increase the flow of blood to that area and this feels good. People say that they feel an increased 'energy flow' there. The stuck place gradually opens up, and feels warmer and more flowing.

This is why scanning the body is so good for our health. It goes into all the dark, hidden, and neglected regions and frees them up. It feels good and I am sure it actually is good. The mind has an instinct to seek out and right imbalances, and you can help it do this when you scan.

Because you notice so much detail when you scan, it's like illuminating the body from within. You go into all the rooms and turn on all the lights. (Of course, some lights are rather dim and some of the bulbs have blown out). It is a small step from here to visualising light, or good energy, flowing through the body, as described in the 'White Light' meditation below.

Some Eastern practices go even further and invite you to actually feel your bones and organs and general anatomy in exquisite detail. This is much more than just a visualisation. If you put the time in, and you're patient, you really can 'see' the liver, the spine, the workings of your inner ear, and the shape they're all in.

THE CHAKRAS

When the mind gets quiet, it has a strong instinct to settle in certain places in the body. If you are scanning through the seven regions described in Chapter 6, it will want to rest in what feels like the centre of those regions. This is what people call the 'chakras' or the 'energy centres'. This is a useful concept if you don't get too mystical about it.

The word 'chakra' means 'wheel', and a wheel has both a hub and a rim. A chakra, therefore, is both the whole network of sensations in a certain region, and the point of balance in the centre. It is all the sensations of life as you perceive them in that part of the body: the lungs moving, the chest rising and falling, the beating of the heart. Nonetheless, people tend to think of the chakra as just the point of balance.

There is a temptation to think of chakras as fixed places in the body, as a kind of spiritual anatomy. In fact, chakras are the network of sensations in a certain place, rather than the place itself. After a race, for example, your heart chakra will be racing and energised. It's quite different if you're just sitting down. If you have a headache on one side of your head, the balance point will be skewed to one side.

People often assume there are seven chakras, because that is the common system used in Yoga. However, the Tibetans work with five chakras, and other systems work with 10 or 28. The Chinese work with a detailed map of the body energies, but they haven't found any chakras. So who is right?

The chakra system is just a template for you to hang your experience on. It can work very well, but realise it is provisional. Just think of a chakra as the network of sensations in an area, and as the balance point in the middle. It's how you personally feel a chakra that matters. If you don't feel it, by definition, it's not there. You can't have an energy centre for non-existent or uncentred sensation.

OPENING THE CHAKRAS

A chakra as a bundle of discrete sensation anywhere in the body, could be big, like the heart chakra, or small, like the sensations in your hand. Your pains are the most obvious chakras of all.

As you scan, you're likely to find parts of the body that feel sore or tight or bound up. Even if there're not obviously painful, they still don't feel particularly good. This is what people refer to as 'blocked energy'.

As I mentioned earlier, when you focus on an area, it usually opens up. It feels warmer, more flowing and expansive, and has a better energy to it. This is why people often go through the body, 'opening up the chakras'.

They usually just go systematically through the seven classical chakras. It's possible to do this purely as a visualisation without actually feeling those regions much at all. If you're more physical and tactile about it, it's more thorough. The process usually goes something like this:

When you're tense and excited, you usually can't find the balance point for the simple reason that the energy isn't balanced anyway. So you have to look at the broader network of sensations first. You need to loosen up all the little imbalances and tensions first, before the mind can settle.

As you relax more, you feel drawn to the central point, or what people usually think of as the chakra. Strange to say, when you find it, there's nothing there. It's just a clear, still, tranquil space, like the eye in the centre of the cyclone. It's small at first and gradually expands the deeper you go.

Most people are quite happy if the chakras or the body energies open up to some degree. If, however, you do this practice a lot, and particularly if you can lead a very simple life, the effects can be amazing.

All the obvious blockages in the body dissolve. This feels radiant and blissful, despite the inevitable discomforts of having a body. Your movements become free and harmonious. The body can seem to glow from within, and indeed, radiate light. This is why saints are often shown surrounded by halos. The experience of 'enlightenment' can literally have this radiant quality.

White Light

INSTRUCTIONS

1.   Relax the body and the breath as usual.

2.   Imagine an almost liquid light flowing through the body.
        A soft golden light, like nectar, or milk and honey.
        Or a sparkling crystal light or a cool blue light or a warm
        pink light.

3.   Feel it flowing especially into the painful places.
        Let the light have texture and aroma and even sound.
        You can amplify the effect by saying an affirmation as
        you breathe: "Love" or "Peace" or "Health".

4.   Imagine the light caressing your organs, flesh and bones.
        Feel it going through the brain, the nervous system,
        throat, lungs, heart, intestines, liver, kidneys, sexual
        organs, the spine, buttocks, arms, legs and feet.
        Give each place a little care and love.

5.   Feel the whole body glowing.
        Imagine a cocoon or bubble of light around you.
        Feel the radiance coming from an inner sun in your heart
        chakra.
        Rest in that inner sun.

Chapter twenty-three

Improving your Health

Don't be surprised if your doctor says to you, "Have you considered meditation?" He's not some alternative quack. Each year I teach about 200 people on doctors' referrals.

The doctors are on firm ground when they recommend meditation. They are backed up by hundreds, perhaps thousands, of scientific studies going back decades. I attended a medical conference recently where the doctor who spoke on meditation cited 212 references in his paper.

The jury has delivered its verdict. Meditation is not like the latest wonder herb from the Amazon. It's not a kind of faith healing based on hypnotic suggestion. If you are sick, meditation can help in measurable ways. If you are not sick, meditation will help you stay healthy. It works in two main ways: it helps the body relax quickly and it settles the over-wrought mind.

RESTORING BALANCE

Meditation works because it restores the body to a state of balance. This is called 'homeostasis' when the systems within the body are at rest or asleep. It is called 'allostatic balance' when the systems are more active but operating within sustainable limits. Balance is that state when the muscle tone is just right, the heart and breathing rates are normal, the levels of gastric juices, blood sugar and acidity are within the ideal range, and so on.

The body is quite capable of operating outside the state of balance. We can run a marathon for example, or eat a massive meal without suffering unduly. However, we're stressing those systems in the body when this happens. If they stay stressed for too long, they get damaged and pathologies start to occur. In fact, sickness can be easily defined as a state of imbalance in one or more of the systems in the body.

The body is always striving to return to homeostasis. Not only do systems work best when in balance, but this is also the optimum state for self-repair and growth. The body puts away the groceries, tidies the house and does structural repairs only when we're relaxed during the day or asleep at night. By relaxing when we can during the day and destressing effectively at night, we help the body heal itself.

THE STRESS AND RELAXATION RESPONSES

The role of maintaining balance falls on the autonomic nervous system. This operates via two opposing functions which we can call the stress response and the relaxation response.

The stress response is like pushing the accelerator flat to the floor. We get a lot of speed but run out of gas fast. Adrenalin is the main hormonal instigator. Our muscles tighten, blood pressure and breathing rates rise, digestion stops and we burn a lot of energy fast. This often feels good as long as it doesn't last too long.

During the relaxation response, the reverse happens. Adrenalin levels fade, muscles soften, blood pressure and breathing rates drop and digestion resumes. The systems in the body return to balance and burn energy at a sustainable rate.

Our bodies are extremely good at maintaining balance, so why do we still get unexpectedly sick? In theory, we could be in a balanced state all day long - eating, working, exercising and resting well. If we kept this going all our lives, there is a good chance we would live to a hale and hearty old age.

But, being conscious animals, we frequently ignore the signs of stress and overrule the intelligence of our bodies. We get over-excited and push ourselves to the limits, and lose all concept of a balanced life. Though we often grind to a halt out of exhaustion, we usually don't recover fully before plunging back into the fray.

We can also be mildly stressed for years at a time. Just to be 10% more stressed than you need to be can make you just as prone to middle-aged illness as can periodic extreme stress. Because mild continual stress is so common, we take it as 'normal' and don't realise how insidious it is.

THE EFFECTS OF CHRONIC STRESS

Stress affects every system of the body, pushing them beyond the level of sustainable function. High blood pressure leads to heart disease, and kidney and respiratory failure. High metabolic rates lead to fatigue and cell damage. Muscular tension leads to physical pain and injury and poor circulation. Constricted respiration contributes to asthma and the lung infections that commonly take away the elderly. The disruption to the digestive system leads to gastrointestinal problems.

The immune system in particular suffers when under stress and a poor immune system affects everything. Many diseases seem particularly related to the malfunctioning of the immune system. It is not surprising that stressed people succumb to illnesses that healthy people shrug off lightly. Years of inner warfare have destroyed their defence capabilities.

Within minutes, meditation can temporarily reverse many of the indicators above. It can be even quicker than taking a pill. While you meditate, you're lowering blood pressure and breathing rates, muscle tension, adrenalin production and so.

This can be very beneficial for certain illnesses. Meditation has the most dramatic effects on people suffering from hypertension, insomnia, migraines, chronic pain, digestive and respiratory problems. While it occasionally acts as a miracle cure for a specific illness, it is more valuable in improving total body health. Let me explain how meditation affects the different systems in the body.

THE CARDIOVASCULAR SYSTEM

With some ailments such as cancer, the links between stress and ill-health are somewhat indirect. With cardiovascular problems, however, the dynamics are obvious and the links are clear: stress is a major contributor to heart disease.

The stress response is designed to massively increase the available energy in the bloodstream in preparation for fight-or-flight. The cardiovascular system is the main engine and delivery system for this.

When stressed, the blood becomes thick with energy-laden fatty acids and glycogen. To deliver this to the muscles more rapidly, the heart and breathing rates increase and the veins and arteries constrict. The accelerated heart is now pumping a more viscous fluid through narrower passages much faster than usual.

This alone can kill you if you're vulnerable. In a stroke or heart attack, the blood vessels burst under the sheer pressure alone. A sudden spike of extreme anger or terror can kill you on the spot.

The real damage, however, occurs over years. Increased pressure causes tiny rips in the lining of the arteries. The thicker blood carries semi-solid blobs of fatty acids within it which scour the walls and increase the damage. When damage occurs, blood platelets and fatty acids get under the lining, coagulate and seal the damage. However each piece of repair work is bulky and juts into the passageways, making them narrower and increasing the overall pressure.

The scene is now set for serious damage. A clot will often break loose under pressure and block a small arteriole. Within seconds, all the cells downstream will suffocate and die. These 'micro-deaths' or 'infarcts' are common in older people but can happen in all of us. Of course, if a large clot breaks loose and jams a major artery, we have a heart attack or stroke.

Heart attacks are dramatic, but the real culprit is the years of hypertension which day by day degrades the cardiovascular system. So what can you do to help - besides diet, exercise and drugs? In brief, anything that helps you relax will de-activate the stress response and bring you back into balance. Quite simply, the more relaxed you are during the day, the more you care for your heart and arteries.

THE FAR-REACHING EFFECTS OF A TIGHT MUSCULATURE

The benefits of a supple musculature are almost impossible to overestimate. The muscles of a healthy child are soft, supple and strong. This ability of muscles to expand and contract fully, as they do in a child, is the epitome of good health. Every cell in the body benefits from healthy muscle function.

Chronically tight muscles burn a lot of energy to stay tight, so they get fatigued and we under-use them. Being stiff, they're prone to injury and many of us carry dozens of micro-injuries in places like the lower back.

Healthy muscles are well aerated and supplied with nutrients, because they relax and contract many times a day. In contrast, tight muscles clamp down on the tiny passageways that carry the blood. The tightest parts of a muscle are like a fortified city. When the gates are closed, supplies can't get in and waste products can't get out. The muscle is starved of oxygen and nutrients and poisoned by its own waste products. Such muscles eventually atrophy and die.

It's not just the muscles that suffer. If the thousands of little muscles throughout the body are tight, they impede the flow of oxygen and nutrients through the veins and arteries. This means that *all* the organs of the body, not just the muscles themselves, can suffer from reduced rations. If you are fighting a disease, a tense body is cutting off the supply lines.

Tight muscles also magnify the effects of stress on breathing and digestion. Both these systems operate on a rhythmic contraction and expansion of muscles. When muscles lock into contraction, these systems suffer.

So how does meditation help? It's very simple. Adrenalin raises muscle tone. It makes muscles contract. Meditating reduces adrenalin, and muscle tone returns to normal. Thousands of big and small muscles throughout the body start to soften within seconds of starting to meditate. It's not a mystery. If you feel your face or shoulder muscles starting to droop, you can be confident it's happening elsewhere as well.

THE UPSET STOMACH

When the body goes into fight-or-flight mode, it switches off the digestion system. Secretions of saliva and digestive juices dry up and the muscles in the gut spasm and lock. The shop is closed. Nothing will move until the crisis is felt to have passed.

There is a good reason for this. The process of digestion itself consumes 10-20% of the body's available energy each day. In a perceived crisis, the mind says, "Digestion can wait. We need that energy for action", and it diverts it to the fight-or-flight muscles of the arms and legs.

Digestion will only start again when we relax. Unfortunately, we often stay tense for hours or days at a time. Since this is not an environment suited to digestion, we literally have 'in-digestion', complete with flatulence and discomfort, and a quite accurate perception that food is sitting heavy in our bellies going nowhere.

Hundreds of studies have proven the connection between stress and the gut. Anxious people commonly suffer from ulcers, heartburn, gas, pain, diarrhea and/or constipation. Stress results in excess hydrochloric acid production and disturbs other digestive juices. If you get several of these symptoms regularly, you could say you have Irritable Bowel Syndrome.

One reason for constipation is that peristalsis is inhibited when we are stressed. Peristalsis is the continuous rhythmic expansion and contraction of gut muscles that squeezes food down the tract. When you're tense, however, the whole tubular system locks in contraction and nothing moves.

As soon as you meditate, you can feel yourself reversing this pattern. As you relax you may start salivating more. This is a clear sign that the digestive system is coming back to life. People often have to swallow at a certain point in their meditation. Another sign is a gurgling stomach. People who are constipated often find they are ready for a bowel movement after meditating.

THE IMMUNE SYSTEM UNDER STRESS

The body only repairs itself when you are relaxed during the day, or asleep at night. Stress produces cortisol which is a potent immunosuppressant. It also produces other indicators of reduced immune function which are too complex to detail here.

If you're chronically tense, your muscles will be deprived of oxygen and feel sore. The pervasive low-grade muscle pain that goes with stress makes people stiff in their movements and often physically inactive. This is disastrous for the lymphatic system.

This is an extensive network of tubes and glands which fights infection and removes waste products throughout the body. Unlike the cardiovascular system, it lacks a pump to drive it along. It is completely dependent on adjacent muscular activity to keep the lymph moving. People who are bedridden, for example, often have lymph pooling in their lower body under the influence of gravity.

If the lymphatic system becomes stagnant through inactivity and rigid musculature, it is less capable of fighting disease and is vulnerable to being infected by the pathogens it is trying to destroy. People with cancers, for example, often need their diseased lymph glands removed as well.

Researchers have unfortunately done lots of experiments stressing little animals to death. From this we know how stress affects immune function. The thymus gland, the lymph glands and the spleen all shrink. The adrenal gland, working hard to pump out enough adrenalin, becomes enlarged. The white blood cell count drops.

The immune system is complex and difficult to understand. It's actually a range of semi-autonomous functions. Sometimes it breaks down because it's over-vigilant and starts destroying healthy tissue, as in rheumatoid arthritis. At other times it becomes exhausted and unable to respond quickly enough to combat pathogens (the best time to destroy the enemy is the moment they first appear, before they can get a foothold).

The immune system is like a standing army constantly engaged in guerrilla warfare on the borders. It never rests. Like any army under constant pressure, it get exhausted, runs out of supplies, gets ambushed from behind and lacks time to regroup and consolidate. The epidemiological evidence supports what we know anyway: if you're stressed, you're much more vulnerable to quite mild pathogens like the flu. If this is the case, you'll also be struggling to cope with bigger problems.

THE ROOTS OF FATIGUE

The biological purpose of the stress response is to give us energy to burn. All those muscles are wired up, burning a huge amount of energy that's going nowhere. A bricklayer enjoying his work will actually burn less energy than a chronic worrier who sits in a chair all day.

If we burn energy fast, we burn out. Stress and worry inevitably lead to exhaustion. And while we may collapse into sleep, we're unlikely to sleep well enough or long enough to recover fully. If we wake up feeling awful and then plunge back into the stress zone, the cycle continues.

When we're young, this high energy/low energy cycle can be a character trait that is hard to break. Many young people are dazzlingly vivacious, running on caffeine and excitement, and often succeed initially in their careers because this is part of their self-image. It's who they think they are.

But as the high-energy hormones of youth start their inevitable decline sometime after thirty, such people wonder why they feel so tired all the time. Useful as nutritional supplements, exercise and other lifestyle factors are, they can't mask the underlying problem forever. Such people have been blowing the budget for years.

Meditation is sometimes described as energy conservation. By doing something simple (i.e. focusing), and watching thoughts rather than reacting to them, you save energy. We usually call this being relaxed. The more hours during the day that you're relaxed, the more energy you save.

INSOMNIA

If you're relaxed during the day, you also get maximum benefit from your sleep at night. If you fall asleep from sheer exhaustion, you're likely to be mentally turbulent during the night. People recognize this when they wake at two in the morning with their minds racing.

Meditation helps insomniacs in many ways. It detaches you from thinking before you go to sleep. If you meditate in bed, you'll usually go to sleep rapidly. If you wake in the night, you can detach from the thoughts that are keeping you awake. And even if you fail to fall asleep again, you can be relaxed in that state (or conserving energy) rather than fretting (or burning energy).

Sleep researchers are suggesting that maybe 80% of us, if we exclude the young and the elderly, are constantly sleep deprived. If we want to be healthy, we could all do with more and better quality sleep.

My students often say they have their best sleeps on the night of their meditation class. It is sad, but many of us have to relearn how to sleep and to value our rest. Otherwise we face a lifetime of periodic stress and exhaustion with its accompanying feelings of lethargy, helplessness and despair.

LIVING COMFORTABLY WITH PAIN

Some of my best students are those who suffer chronic pain. They have good motivation to practise and they see the results immediately. They commonly say that meditation is the only thing that is guaranteed to work.

Pain usually has some injury at its base, but stress will enormously amplify the amount of pain you feel. Tense muscles ache because of oxygen deprivation and exhaustion. Since muscles are 40% of our body mass, this translates into pain all over the body and augments the pain of actual injuries.

If we're stressed, nothing in our bodies functions very well. It's not surprising we have stomach pains and headaches and a susceptibility to niggling low-level infections that make us miserable.

Meditation helps immediately with pain because it cleans up our emotional response. Pain and emotion come hand in hand. Any pain we feel is a combination of the injury plus our emotional reaction to it. If we hate, fear or resent the pain, we project those emotions on to it and it feels much worse.

Meditation doesn't get rid of the pain or block it out. These are two impossible scenarios. Instead, it helps us to 'just watch' the pain with detachment. The Stress Reduction Program at the University of Massachusetts has had phenomenal results in reducing patients' perception of pain in this way. If the 'pain' a person feels is 20% pure sensation and 80% emotional amplification, then watching the pain as sensation alone completely changes its character.

RELIEVING STRESS AND ANXIETY

If you don't relax adequately, you feel habitually tense. If this continues over months and years, the physical discomfort alone can push you into chronic anxiety. Eventually, you may start to have panic attacks, when you feel you can't cope with the simplest things (which is true). If this continues, you may be heading for a nervous breakdown or a serious illness.

In a recent class, I had three state managers from different firms. When I asked why they wanted to learn meditation, the first said, "I can barely cope any longer". The second said, "I had a heart attack at thirty-eight". The third said, "I had a nervous breakdown seven months ago".

Meditation, as the art of relaxing consciously, is the perfect antidote for extreme stress, even though lifestyle changes may also be necessary. I doubt if any other stress management strategy, minute for minute, works as well as meditation. I find that high achievers, being naturally diligent, learn the skill quite rapidly.

Meditation also works well for performance anxiety. Musicians, sports people, students and anyone who has to put on a performance at work, need to monitor their tension/relaxation levels well. I've helped several musicians and sports people achieve their best with the help of meditation.

For example, I helped one young singer prepare for a national competition. She told me her tension levels would peak too early, so she'd be tired by the time she went on stage. Learning to manage her tension levels helped her to win the competition, which boosted her career enormously.

Anxiety, panic and phobias are all results of the stress response locked in overdrive. I often teach clients in conjunction with their psychologists or psychiatrists. Our work is beautifully complementary. They help their clients to a cognitive understanding of their problem, while I help them reverse the physical effects in their bodies. If our clients can wind their tension levels down from 90% of maximum to 70%, they are much less likely to suffer panic attacks or succumb to phobias. It has been very gratifying to see people extract themselves from states of extreme misery in this way.

As we age, we become less resilient to stress, but our stress levels typically climb as the years go by. The rational worry that goes with living in an uncertain world spills over into toxic worry about things that don't matter, or things we can't control. We try to cope with demanding situations by cranking up the energy. If we try really hard and work long hours, we feel safer than if we relax and take it easy. Our habitual tension level - the rate at which we burn energy - moves a few notches higher.

Before we realise it, we can be running very close to the panic mark all the time we are awake. A few years like this, usually in our thirties and forties, seriously depletes our inner resources. All it takes is one extra outer stress and you're thrown over the line. You explode at the kids or take stress leave or fall ill or suffer a nervous breakdown.

Usually, you're flummoxed by the situation. Your strategy when under pressure has always been to push harder, and you can see what that has led to. You can't just make some little adjustment and get back on track. It often requires a change in self-image and values, and a willingness to listen compassionately to the needs of your body.

HELPING WITH CHRONIC ILLNESS

We occasionally hear of 'miracle' cures through meditation, and there is little doubt that they do occur. People boast, 'Five years ago, the doctors gave me six months to live, but I'm still here'. To be fair to the doctors, they're usually quite accurate in their predictions but they work on the law of averages. There will always be those at the extremes who unexpectedly recover from (and unexpectedly succumb to) an illness.

So what was the secret of those who unexpectedly recovered? This is notoriously hard to pin down, but they usually have a healthy and well-balanced optimism that doesn't slip into denial. Furthermore, they commonly take control of their treatment and make lifestyle changes to support the process.

Meditation can be a linchpin to these changes. At the very least, it helps you cope with pain and distress. It also helps you see the dramas around your illness with some detachment and emotional control.

Nonetheless, its direct physical benefits remain enormous. People with cancer often ask me, "How can I boost my immune system?" This question usually comes with the rather simplistic attitude that positive thoughts will help rally the troops.

Meditation acts in a more comprehensive way. The battle between the immune system and an illness is a drawn-out war of attrition, like World War II. Victory goes to the side with greater industrial capacity and access to raw materials. The wins and losses occur on the front line, but the war is actually won in the factories and farms and scientific laboratories.

While meditation has specific effects on the immune system, its real benefits are much wider. Meditation improves blood circulation and heart function, and will help you digest your food better, sleep better, cope with pain and distress better and enjoy life more despite your illness.

If your body as a whole is functioning in a healthy and relaxed manner, it's got the resources to fight a specific illness. Since meditation, with its ability to restore and maintain a general state of homeostasis, acts as the command post, this may be all you need to turn around a serious illness.

If you do something like the breath meditation well, you'll get most of the health benefits mentioned above. On the other hand, if you try a positive visualisation without first establishing a good base of calm and clarity, the results will be disappointing.

As a rule-of-thumb, we can say the bodyscanning practices tend to work best. They enhance your awareness of how your body and mind function, and that can have remarkable results.

It can also be useful to tailor-make a meditation for a certain illness. You can find some of these in my other book, 'Why Meditation is Good for your Health'. You can also consult with me privately or by phone or email, if you wish.

MEDITATING FOR A BETTER QUALITY OF LIFE

Stress and ill-health can make you look at your quality of life. If you're too young to retire, at least you can take time to smell the roses. Meditation, by enhancing the sensing function and bringing you into the moment, makes you do just this.

For many people, 'meditation' is less a formal practice than a reminder to slow down, relax and enjoy what they are doing. They try to integrate the qualities of awareness and being present in all that they do.

I find that older people who learn to detach from a lifetime of worry, often become passionate about some new activity or study. It becomes their meditation, relaxing and inspiring them. Whether it's a sport or a study or an art, it has the same quality of internal satisfaction as meditation, rather than the external rewards of money or status.

Chapter twenty-four

A Natural
Psychotherapy

Meditation is obviously good for our health, but how does it help with our mental pain? And can it go further and give us the deep happiness and bliss described in the Asian literature? Even people who meditate for panic attacks or insomnia feel that meditation can offer more than symptom relief.

Twenty-four hours a day, our bodies are working for self-repair and maximum function. It seems that the mind has just the same instinct for health and balance as the body. In fact, the process of mental healing is just as systematic and thorough as the way the body cleans up illnesses and repairs wounds.

The best way to support this process is to be passively aware, and to do as little as possible. The body repairs itself best when we are relaxed or asleep. Similarly the mind works best if we can just stand back and let the process happen without interfering. This is why a retreat, which is largely an opportunity to be undisturbed and do nothing for a long time, can have such healthy psychological effects.

CHOOSING OUR RESPONSE

Over time, meditation works like therapy. It clears the mental garbage and leads to a well-grounded happiness. The process is quiet and subtle but very thorough, and it does much the same work as traditional therapy. Unfortunately, we can't make the mind healthy just by wishing it. We do have to clear out the garbage first and most of us would rather do anything but that.

Meditation changes the way we react to things. It's easy to blame our hectic modern lives or our miserable jobs or our lack of money for our unhappiness, but all of this is secondary. Some people can be serene and joyful in a concentration camp. Others are paralysed by anxiety in the midst of trouble-free lives. Whether we live in Heaven or Hell depends largely on our response to what happens to us.

Living is often painful. We all carry wounds - big, small and invisible - and are hurt, to some degree, almost every day. The art of living is to willingly accept the pain we can't avoid. This usually takes decades to learn.

Often our misery is caused by years of unresolved anxiety, anger and desire. Because meditation calms us down, it gives us the chance to see how troubled we are. It also gives us the space to gently and thoroughly loosen those stuck emotions.

COMPROMISING OUR EMOTIONAL EXPRESSION

Hardly any of us act with the emotional freedom of a two-year-old. To be civilized human beings, we often have to repress our emotions and pretend to things we don't feel. We also need the shock response, which enables us to go emotionally numb to cope with a crisis.

We all need to be able to put feelings on hold until we can release them safely. Unfortunately, we often don't release them at all. We prefer to appear cool, capable and always in control. We lock our messy feelings in the basement and try to forget about them.

Unfortunately we can only postpone their expression. The emotions won't go away and die. They wait in the basement with a lifetime's worth of other buried feelings for any chance to emerge. They continually seep back into consciousness as unwanted moods or psychosomatic pains. This is when we over-react to minor events, or just feel bad without knowing why.

Emotions are very physical things. The word 'e-motion' literally means 'to move out'. Feelings want to move from the core of our body either upwards, as in the case of anger or joy, or downwards, as in the case of fear or sorrow.

If we don't block our feelings, they move through easily and equilibrium returns. We see this pattern of tension and release occur very quickly in little children. It is however like a storm or a fever. It will incapacitate us while it's happening. A person giving way to grief, anger or desire is temporarily uncivilized. He or she is unable to go to work or get the kids off to school.

So we freeze our emotion by tensing the body. This stops it moving through at all. Much of our tension is the effort to suppress or control unwanted emotion. Unfortunately, the deep freeze eventually overloads and breaks down, usually in our middle years.

I once analysed a dream in which exactly this image arose. A woman dreamt that her refrigerator had broken down. When she looked in the freezer she found the dismembered corpse of her estranged husband. It was starting to thaw. She would have to take each piece out with her hands to dispose of it.

She realized this related to the way she 'froze up' years earlier. She left her husband because she couldn't cope with his wasting sickness, and felt bad about this. She also thought this might be the cause of her recurring skin cancers. It was now seven years later and she was emotionally stronger. It was time to take out the corpse of those frozen feelings and loosen her habit of emotional suppression.

AWARENESS IS THE BEST THERAPY

It is a psychological axiom that a patient has to become aware of his trauma to be healed. A therapist rarely 'gets rid of' a patient's childhood trauma, for example. She just enables the client to see it with clarity and detachment. For some reason, and it's still not clear why, this awareness alone does the trick.

Meditation operates the same way. As we sit in silence, our subtle discontents and confusion inevitably come to the surface. By not running away from them, we are learning to watch them all with increasing calm and detachment.

It starts with the distractions. Every meditator knows that when you try first to focus, you're likely to get distracted. You find yourself thinking about work or food or money or last night's TV. Your body feels tired and sore and you don't like the scratchy mood you're in. You feel all these 'distractions' are undermining your meditation.

In fact, you could say, like Shakespeare, "Sweet are the uses of adversity that feelingly persuade me who I am". This mental clutter is who you are in this moment. You can't push it away. You only relax when you can accept the full complexity of who you are and what you are feeling in that moment.

I particularly notice this in my evening classes. Someone bustles into the room after work, hyped up and cheerful. Five minutes into the meditation, she realises she's actually quite exhausted and irritable.

Though she resents it, as she acknowledges how she's feeling, she starts to unwind. After fifteen minutes she's more balanced and in touch with herself. In a single meditation she goes from chaos to acceptance to some degree of peace.

LAYERS OF DISCONTENT

Typically, the immediate problems arise first. Your body feels exhausted and vaguely unwell. Your thoughts are buzzing around unfinished business at work or home. You realise you're not coping very well emotionally. Of course, you also have lovely times as you meditate, but the gritty bits inevitably come through as well.

In time, the deeper layers of discontent will also emerge. Typically we resist them at first. When we finally admit their presence in the mind, it's rather like boils surfacing on the skin and bursting. They can release quite rapidly.

Typically, the big traumas of the past, such as a marriage failure or the death of a relative, come through in thousands of bite-sized pieces. The mind is very kind. It waits till you're calm and feeds you only what you can handle. Instead of one big breakthrough, you get hundreds of small memories or feelings that can pass in seconds.

It's subtle but very deep and thorough. It covers exactly the same ground as any good therapy but more quietly. A therapist provides a safe container and 'adult' perspective to help a client face painful things without repression. Meditation provides the same support by laying a strong base of calm and clarity.

When you're calm, you're not burning much energy. The fires are low. This means that when a feeling of sadness or anger arises, there's not much agitation in the body to fuel it. As the habitual stories around an issue arise, you can stay cool and see them for what they are - just stories.

This is why there's such an emphasis on tranquility in meditation. When you feel good and in control, you don't need to suppress sadness and anger the way we normally do. You can relax around them and let them move through.

The more calm and clear the mind is, the faster the process works. Paradoxically, the more you relax, the more emotion you're able to feel without being overwhelmed. You feel a greater range of emotions and they move through fast. Once you understand the process, it's quite awesome. Whenever the mind is strong and spacious, it will throw out more of the inner toxins, just as the body does when it's fasting.

TOXINS CAN EMERGE AS PHYSICAL SENSATIONS

Often when you meditate, you strike resistance. The mind squirms, trying to avoid or get rid of some discomforting thought or feeling. If you assume meditation is only about feeling good, you may think you're not doing it right and you stop. This is a mistake. The meditation is actually bearing fruit.

Toxic material can emerge in three obvious ways: as body sensation, as pure feeling or as imagery. Physically you may feel discomfort, itchiness, nausea, muscle tremors, shooting pains, flushes, agitation and so on. These are typically quite faint but uncomfortable nonetheless. Something feels vaguely wrong inside though you can't put your finger on it.

Eventually, you realise that these discomforts are worse because you're unconsciously trying to suppress them. Usually there is some small, sticky emotion around them that you don't like. If you can accept the emotion, however, the sensations usually free up.

Occasionally there are memories or images locked within the sensations. One student told me of painful tightness in her upper arms when she meditated. I suggested it might be a physical memory emerging. A few days later she got the pictures. When she was a child, her mother used to rebuke her by grabbing her by the forearms and shaking her violently.

On another occasion a woman said she kept getting images of spots of blood on bathroom tiles. Eventually she remembered what it was about. When she was nine she found her mother dead in the bath - she had slit her wrists. As a child my student had coped as she naturally would, by repressing many of her reactions. With the maturity of an adult, she was able to revisit that territory.

However, most emotions emerge without accompanying pictures. Some are obviously anger, resentment, despair or fear, but many are just the queasy, off-colour, awkward, indefinable moods that seem to come and go without any reason. Whatever is happening, the basic instructions don't change: just watch it all with detachment.

In time we get to know ourselves and our body/mind rhythms very well. This can be quite a revelation. We are often not at all who we thought we were, or who we are supposed to be. We may notice emotions, images and thoughts that are completely unlike our usual sense of self.

The Swiss psychologist Jung calls this 'integrating the shadow', though more often it's an acknowledgement of conflicting inner voices and feelings. Strange as all this can be, it's grounding and illuminating to recognize it. No wonder our psyche is rather turbulent at times! No wonder we can't dominate it all with our conscious minds.

BLISS AND TRANCE

Meditation can also make you feel very, very good, and the benefits of this are impossible to overestimate. It can also happen very quickly. One student after his very first class said, "I've been searching for this peace for 50 years and here it is!"

Meditation allows you to disengage from your thoughts and relax at will. If you're a driven, anxious, obsessive person, this ability alone could turn your life around. If you're sick or confused or your life is an inescapable mess, meditation can still gives you times of perfect peace and beauty. Meditation, just by enabling you to relax and calm the mind, is one of the simplest routes out of unremitting misery.

But it also goes much further than that. There is no pleasure on earth to compare with the bliss, or 'samadhi', of a deep meditation. I know this seems an extravagant claim, but meditators will know what I'm talking about. It's impossible to describe it adequately. It resembles the heights of love, or the joy of intellectual or physical accomplishment but, unlike these, it can also be endlessly repeated.

In deep states, we leave our sense of self behind. You barely know who or what you are. All that remains is pure consciousness, and it's utterly radiant and blissful. It can be profoundly tranquil or rich in visions. We might logically assume that the absence of our usual thoughts would be a dull and unconscious state, but it's not. It's lovely beyond imagining.

In this state, unhealthy emotions vanish utterly, like snowflakes in a fire. With no self to defend, all fear and anger disappear. All desire and craving for other things vanish. No aversion or attraction of any kind can sway your mind. All that remains is effortless love and acceptance.

Paradoxically, this happens only when 'you' stop trying to achieve it. If you want something, both 'you' and the desire are in the mind, so absorption can't arise. "Don't try to awaken", as they say in Zen. "Just sit". You drop into absorption when the last of the subtle attractions and aversions vanishes.

Once you drop into the object, a strange thing can happen. The object vanishes also. There is simply infinite space and bliss.

Originally, you were one with the object. Now you are one with nothing. You are like a cat at a mouse hole, intensely alert. But even the cat has gone. This is the first stage of trance. You have merged into the background vibration of pure consciousness itself. Actually, it is always there, like the background hum of the Big Bang resonating through the universe.

In this state, the mind becomes unified. The psychic energy, usually scattered into a thousand thoughts, now streams up and down the spinal column. This can be felt as an almost liquid light. It is described as the nectar of the gods, or like 'sugar cane juice', melting the bound energies in the central channel.

When the mind unifies, nothing is excluded. You may feel one with God, with Nature and with all that lives. You are no longer at war with yourself or anyone or anything. Even your suffering is perfect in its own way. Nothing is lacking. What more could you possibly want?

Of course, it would be nice to stay in that state longer than we do. It rarely lasts more than a few seconds or minutes, but its after-effects can be enormous. It is an extremely healthy and life-giving state. This is when cancers may start to dissolve or the buried grief and anger of decades may disintegrate. This is our first glimpse of Paradise and, according to the great mystics, the only place we will ever find it.

The feeling you find in deep states then flows back into ordinary consciousness and becomes another kind of love. We're better able to face everything that enters our minds and lives with an open heart. We can accept every thought, feeling, sensation, and experience just as they are, without wishing them otherwise. Many of these are still hard and bitter, but we no longer feel crushed by them. We've found the secret of happiness inside, and we don't need to seek it externally.

Chapter twenty-five

The Many Flavours
of Meditation

People often say to me, "I've been meditating for months but I don't know if I've reached it yet". They usually assume that meditation is a state of blissful emptiness, and this rarely happens for them. If you regard entry into paradise as the sign of a successful meditation, you are bound to fail most of the time. It's not a good ideal.

So is meditation an ideal state you strive to attain, or is it a variety of states sharing common traits? Beginners typically believe the first, while skilled meditators know it is the second. In this chapter, I'll explain the different kinds of patterns your meditation could fall into, including the useless ones. I'll also give you ways to evaluate your practice.

THE 'PERFECT' MEDITATION

Sometimes you go into a beautiful state and you know, "That's it! That's what I want! This is real meditation. Now I know how to do it." But as the Buddhists say, "If you want something badly, it's bound to make you miserable", and, damn it all, they're right! For the next ten sittings you struggle to get back there and fail.

This 'perfect' state will appear often enough if your skills are adequate. We usually get glimpses of it in most sessions. It is tranquil because the body becomes very still as it goes into stage one sleep.

It's blissful because you're still awake enough to enjoy it.

In contrast with the densely packed thoughts of waking life, the mind feels vast and empty. Nonetheless, there can be a delicate effervescence of images and embryonic thoughts within the emptiness. This is why it feels blissful rather than blank.

Typically, you slip in and out of this state fairly rapidly. You touch it for a few seconds, then you're just as quickly out of it. Most people are very happy just to be in its vicinity. As soon as a beginner has moments of clear wakefulness at the edge of sleep, she'll taste it. The only difference between her and more skilled meditators is that they can string more seconds together before slipping out of it.

Even this state comes with variations. If you can slip down a notch into unconsciousness, the very slow delta waves start appearing. If you're good at this, you don't fall off the chair, but the mind really has gone blank.

With skill, this can be a deeper meditation, but more commonly it's a kind of controlled sleep. People emerge saying, "I don't know where I was the last few minutes", and they're usually quite pleased with themselves. Monks or people on long retreats often use this state to recuperate, and usually need less sleep at night as a result.

SOME TYPICAL MEDITATIONS

A typical meditation goes through three stages: tense, relaxing and relaxed. These relate to the brainwave states of beta, alpha and theta. The first stage is the busy beta state, actively chasing thoughts. The second stage is the relaxing alpha state, more sensually oriented and inclined to wander. The third stage is theta, where you are slipping into sleep with a sense of space, abandonment of self, and occasional dream imagery.

Strange to say, the most useful is alpha, the state in the middle. Here you are focused but still aware of background thoughts and sensations. You learn to detach from thoughts and watch them from a distance. This is where you do the spade work and get the mind clean.

If you've had a shocking day and the mind is wild, your meditation may feel messy and unsatisfying. Yet the messiest meditations are often the most productive. When you disconnect from the worst garbage, you can relax quite rapidly. You may not feel happy or serene, but you'll be in a much healthier state afterwards. If you're really agitated, you may not even approach theta, and yet just the shift from beta to alpha would make this a 'good' meditation.

Some people virtually bypass the alpha state. They collapse from red-alert into sleep within a minute of sitting down. It's not very elegant, and but it may be exactly what they need. They're probably exhausted and suffering sleep deprivation as well. These people benefit most from very short, but frequent, meditations during the day.

THINKING WHILE YOU MEDITATE

Most meditators have a dark secret. Although we know thinking is 'bad' when we meditate, we all do it. We can't resist it. The art is to control and contain it.

Most thinking undermines our mental clarity and relaxation. It spends the capital we're accumulating. Yet we all do little bursts of thinking when we sit. Although this apparently goes against the rules, it's too useful to resist. When you relax, you often see a problem from a different angle. "Of course! That's the answer", you think, and you process it a little.

When you're relaxed, you think very differently. It's more like watching the mind think. You let it do the work for you. An issue arises and you watch your thoughts and associations dance around it. It's a kind of lateral, quick-firing, non-linear thinking.

This works better the more you relax. You know you're getting caught in thoughts when you feel the body tightening. At the sleep threshold, the quality of thought gets even finer. In particular, the mind will think in images rather than words.

Even the best of meditators will do some thinking when they meditate. No one goes on a three-month retreat just to become tranquil. They also want to sort a few things out while they're there. This is why we meditate, after all: to relax and think more clearly.

HOW TO THINK SAFELY

Firstly, I recommend that you at least acknowledge when you're thinking. Since it often takes place quietly in the background, you can pretend it's not happening or that it doesn't matter. It's much better to process a thought consciously than to semi-consciously chew it over for minutes.

Secondly, when you think on a subject, spend as little time as possible on it. A few sentences will do. Don't try to finish it off. Be willing to let it go rapidly. Be miserly with your attention.

Thirdly, remain in touch with the breath or the body. If you're half with the thinking and half with the body, you won't get swept away so easily. Check the body every ten seconds or so for signs of rising tension.

Fourthly, relax before you let yourself think. If you try to process thoughts while you're still in beta, you'll never even get to alpha. The quality of thought improves exponentially the deeper you relax. Thinking while at the edge of sleep can be very inspired.

EVALUATING YOUR MEDITATION

If you assume that a meditation must always feel good, you'll often fail. If you are ill or in pain or distressed or on medication or your life is in turmoil, your meditation will highlight that. It will give you more balance and perspective and relax your body, but it won't work as a happy pill or a pain-killer.

While you try to steer the meditation as best you can, the outcome largely depends on factors beyond your control: how stressed or relaxed or exhausted you are to start with; your state of health and the kind of day you've had; the amount of available time you've got; the chronic problems affecting you; how long since your last meditation, and so on.

Personally, I just do my best when I meditate and I accept what turns up. It's invariably a mirror to my state of mind and health at that moment. A meditation could be deep or shallow or wild or serene or bizarre or humdrum. Personally, I like this uncertainty.

Although I do have goals when I meditate, the biggest is self-acceptance and seeing things 'just as they are'. It's not that easy to say 'yes' to all my passing moods and sensations, but it's very satisfying when I can. In contrast, I'm quite suspicious of my efforts at self-improvement. I find this invariably involves tension, aversion and longing to some degree. It rarely leads to a good outcome.

"AM I REALLY MEDITATING?"

You can't answer this question unless you know what you're trying to do. If you're striving for the perfect experience, then the answer will often be 'no'. If, however, you're trying to relax the body and make the mind clearer, the situation is quite different.

The best way to check is to ask, "Am I more relaxed, and is the mind clearer than when I started?" There should be no mystery about this. If you've trained yourself to recognize the physical signs of relaxation, you can assess that objectively.

Similarly, it shouldn't be hard to assess whether the mind is clearer. It's unlikely to be blank, but it's probably moving more slowly and deliberately. You can direct it more easily, and the thoughts will have a lower emotional charge behind them. This is a clearer and more workable mind.

You can also ask yourself during the sitting, "Am I focused?" If you've lost your meditation object, you'd have to wonder. I'd suggest that you're meditating only when you're consciously focused or consciously watching the mindstream.

On the other hand, if you're sitting in a pleasant dreamy state, you're just relaxing. This is a healthy state but it's not meditating. People often space out, daydream and fall asleep when they 'meditate'. They can get defensive about this, saying, "Isn't this what meditation is about? Being relaxed?"

Meditation is a relaxed and *alert* state. Meditation implies relaxation, but relaxation doesn't imply meditation. Any time we sit, we'll actually alternate between these two. In those moments when we're consciously focused and watching, we're meditating. When we're losing it a bit and drifting away, we're just relaxed.

Why is this important anyway? If you check, you'll find it's only the moments you're actually meditating that do the work. That's the engine. When you're just relaxing, you're dissipating the results.

If you did a sitting where you were meditating 50% of the time and just relaxing the other 50%, that would be a good sitting. Occasionally you have a stunning session where you crank it up to a 90% to 10% ratio. If the ratio shifts the other way and you just sit in a daze of dreamy thoughts, you're likely to give up meditating pretty soon. It'll be unsatisfying and finally not worth the time.

The most time-efficient meditations are the short ones. It's easy to be well-focused for most of a two-minute meditation. But if you sit for an hour, the average quality could be very poor. In fact a good 15-minute sitting can have as much actual meditation in it as an undisciplined hour-long sitting.

Years of training has made me appreciate the benefits of discipline. Even in the deepest states, I try to hold my focus, though I frequently change it as well. And I always aim for the highest quality of dispassionate awareness and check how it fluctuates. Sometimes I check the quality several times a minute. In those times when my mind is vague, I just do the best I can without criticising myself. If I'm clear, I enjoy it without getting attached to it.

WHY MEDITATION MAY FAIL TO WORK

Meditation is a relatively simple and clear skill. Unfortunately many people get mediocre results with it. I have seen many long time meditators who are not happy or well-balanced people.

Firstly, meditating just to relax will always have limited value. People who feel that meditation should involve letting go of all effort will miss the point. It takes a little discipline to cut loose from thoughts. If you think of meditation as a kind of daydreaming or oblivion, you'll waste a lot of time.

People understand about focusing, but many don't know about awareness. It's like trying to fly with one wing. They are forever trying to block out thoughts and failing unless all the conditions are right. Focusing by itself only works if you've got something big to tune into, such as chanting in a group or a physical activity.

For the same reason, many people can only meditate in the special atmosphere of religious or personal development groups, with someone leading them by the hand. This is meditation as a kind of voluntary hypnosis. But once you walk out the door, or you stop chanting, you can no longer meditate. It's a place-specific experience, not a portable skill.

Even experienced meditators can fail to understand the basic skills. They can sit for hours counting the breaths, but without really focusing on them. They are relaxed but lost in an endless stream of quiet thinking.

The results of regularly sitting like this can be worse than no meditation at all. You may be giving yourself an hour a day to do nothing but think. Some meditators are addicted to introspection and self-analysis.

POOR HELP

Meditation is basically a self-therapy, and therapies work best with a specialist to reality-check you and puncture your self-deceptions. In theory a meditation teacher should do this. In practice, it almost never happens. The students don't report and the teacher is too busy to ask.

Meditation teachers usually act as ABC instructors or as spiritual leaders, but not as therapists or guides. They may not know your name or anything about you, but they will boldly tell you what to do. They don't tune into you personally, as a counselor would.

Most Western teachers have incomplete training or none at all, apart from their own experience. Many have just attended a few retreats or workshops and taken it from there. They often teach just one technique to everyone.

In contrast, a Burmese teacher was expected to have ten years' training before he started to teach. He learnt a range of practices for different situations and personality types. It also takes a long time to understand the trickiness of the mind. Unfortunately the Asian teachers usually lack what we would regard as good teaching skills: they generally preach or lecture instead. Although you can glean much of use from such teachers, you eventually have to figure things out on your own.

Chapter twenty-six

Meditation Plus

Is meditation all you need? Is a discipline that gives you a calm, clear and self-reflective mind sufficient in itself? The Buddha thought so. He said that you don't need religious or philosophic beliefs, a teacher or a tradition. You don't even need him! If your eye is clear, you'll know what to do. Your inner confusion will go, and no one can fool you.

However, meditation itself is so simple and versatile that it blends easily with many disciplines. Just as water is the basic ingredient of whisky, fruit juice, herbal teas and sport drinks, so meditation mixes with many other activities and is often confused with them. It's rare to find meditation in an unadulterated form.

Like water, a calm clear mind doesn't have a strong flavour. Meditation invariably takes its flavour from the setting or the teacher or the philosophy in which you meet it, or the purpose for which you do it. These can completely overwhelm the meditation component within them.

If you're meditating for spiritual purposes or to improve your life or to heal your body and soul, you may forget to relax adequately or to get the mind clear first. If you don't develop these basic skills, then the results will be patchy, no matter how important your aspirations are.

Yet if you master the skill, it's possible that everything else may fall into place anyway. It's good to remember that meditation as a skill is something quite distinct from the many purposes it's used for.

In this chapter, I examine how meditation is used as part of other disciplines, since this is how you will usually encounter it. Sometimes it fits well, and sometimes it doesn't. Meditation in itself is almost always benign. Misused, it can lead to fantasy and dependence and cost you a lot of money. The hype and promises around it can be vast, while the actual meditation training you receive may be so tacky and juvenile as to be almost useless.

MEDITATION AND YOGA

Meditation combines well with any kind of body work or exercise, and especially with yoga. Yoga and the martial arts have deep connections with meditation, and may well be the first place you meet it.

I've done yoga on and off for thirty years, and usually do two or three hours a day if I'm on retreat. It has worked very well for me. Yoga, by stretching the muscles, is the exact antidote to tension, which of course contracts them. It also trains you in very precise body awareness, which is a huge advantage when you meditate.

Of course there is more to yoga than stretching. This is where the overlaps between meditation and other disciplines get confusing. Yoga may or may not include meditation. However, it is quite likely to be a lifestyle discipline involving philosophic and religious beliefs.

SELLING HOPE

Meditation is frequently found in combination with inspirational ideas, hopes and beliefs. In our consumer culture, many groups are clamouring for our minds and money. It is a huge business. Hope is a very saleable commodity, as the success of the great religions has demonstrated.

Sometimes our hopes are satisfied by adopting a religious path. More commonly nowadays, we buy or do or attend things in the hope or belief that we'll benefit. We can't check the hard facts about whether they work or not, because they're usually unverifiable anyway.

Meditation, belief and hope are frequently found together. When you meditate at a monastery or New Age gathering or a self-development course, how much are you relaxing because of the meditation and how much because of the inspiring ideas? And does it matter, if it makes you feel good?

Research has shown that people who believe in anything at all are commonly happier and healthier than those who don't. There are health risks to being a sceptic. But those beliefs might not have any connection to reality, and illusions have a habit of biting you in the end.

Believing in itself relieves stress. Belief and hope bring order and a road map to a chaotic world and therefore relieve anxiety. In other words, they have the same physiological effects as meditation: they help you relax and feel good. And they can be addictive.

Yet this mixture of meditation and hope is often a mismatch. At bottom, meditation works differently. It grounds you in reality. It puts you face to face with the raw data of your own feelings and sensations in the moment. It gives you a deep sense of your own truth and individuality which is largely beyond ideologies.

Systems that involve hope and belief, however, often involve a flight into fantasy and possibilities. By definition, they can't be tested. Typically, testimonials and claims take the place of evidence, and any rational analysis is discouraged.

I suspect that belief systems benefit from incorporating meditation, but not vice versa. If meditating is part of your religious practice or self-development program, you are likely to understand the ideas in more depth. However, your basic meditative qualities of relaxation and clarity of mind may not improve at all.

CULTS ARE NOT WHAT THEY SEEM

If you learn meditation in a Christian or Buddhist or Hindu setting, you know there's a religious aspect to it. It's above board.

You know what the deal is. This is what distinguishes a religion from a cult.

Cults however are masters of deception. The vast majority don't look like cults at all. They operate like the Mafia, behind false fronts. Most are not religious at all. They just exploit your spiritual hunger or emotional confusion to get at your money.

Cults operate on deceptive advertising. Some will be obviously cultist or way-out, but they're much more likely to present themselves as fitness classes or self-development courses or study groups or as educational institutes or weight loss programs or staff management regimes or pyramid selling schemes. Anything that offers you a new and inspiring belief to improve your life could be a cult. At some point you realise you've spend a lot of money and time and got very little.

It's good to realise that meditation is frequently used as bait. "Come to our free meeting and learn to meditate". Many famous yoga schools are religious groups that run yoga classes primarily to recruit members. The biggest challenge for any religion or cult, or just anyone trying to make money, is, "How do you get people in the door?" Once they're in, and you've got them feeling good about themselves, the rest is easy.

MEDITATION OFTEN LEADS TO DEPENDENCY

Cults and lifestyle businesses frequently use meditation and similar devices to put people into hypnotic and suggestible states. It can happen very easily. If you talk at an audience for an hour, about half will be in a light hypnotic state by the end. They'll be relaxed because they're doing nothing.

Their critical faculties will largely be cut off by the speaker's words. They'll be prone to suggestion, so what the speaker says seems plausible. They're much more likely to sign up for the workshop or buy the product afterwards.

Religions and cults are very good at inducing this relaxed, suggestible state. It's the secret of their success. In Hindu gatherings, you typically sing songs before the guru speaks. Many churches do much the same. Any kind of body movement like yoga or tai chi will also get you out of your head. A leader speaking in an incantatory way or guiding a meditation works perfectly. People love it and keep coming back for more.

Even if you just attend a group in someone's home, the meditation you do there can induce dependency. It's a relaxed, uncritical state that feels good. In a group setting, it's often hypnotically induced by subtle directions, past associations and non-verbal hints. And guided meditations are often designed to suggestively reshape the way you think anyway.

Even the smallest and most benign of groups has its unspoken direction and values. If you're dependent on the group to meditate at all, you may feel obliged or be persuaded to take them on board.

Though meditation in its essence is as bland as water, it always takes on a flavour from the way you encounter it. In time, however, you should find your own flavour. It should taste of you. If you don't know how to find and sustain this inner taste, you're likely to stay with the flavour of the group.

Of course, the group ideology may be exactly what you want. You will be meditating, but it is meditation plus. You can combine it with spiritual healing or mind-power training or Tibetan Buddhism or restructuring your thought patterns or developing your financial skills or doing compassionate work or making the chi flow, and so on. Just remember that meditation, as the art of relaxing the body and clearing the mind, is not exactly the same as any of these. You need to know what you want.

SELF-DEVELOPMENT

Meditation has close links with the great traditions of self-development towards the perfection of the mind. In Burma the monk is expected to go through a sequence of verifiable experiences over the years. A Tibetan will commit himself to lifetimes perfecting the virtues essential for awakening.

A Tibetan professor, rather like a Catholic priest, was expected to contemplate the doctrine for decades, until he was utterly convinced of its truth and could convincingly argue it with others. Christian, Islamic, Judaic, and shamanic traditions, plus countless smaller mystery cults, map out stages in the development of the perfect human being. Common to most of these is intense self-analysis and acknowledgement of one's shortcomings, and an image of the perfection that you strive to achieve.

In all these systems it is hard to distinguish meditation as a healthy and natural path of inner growth from forms of self-indoctrination. There is no doubt that despite their great antiquity, they utterly fail many people who enter them. There are miserable and defeated priests and monks the world over.

The same is probably true of modern self-development regimens that are not overtly religious. Freudian psychoanalysis, for example, is based on unverifiable or false hypotheses and demands submission to the superior wisdom of the analyst (disagreement is called 'resistance'). It also promises the earth, costs a fortune and works very poorly as a therapy, as many studies have shown.

Nonetheless, its enormous financial success has inspired many imitators. New therapies and self-development regimens appear every year, each with their own extravagant claims and unverifiable premises. When such systems are criticised for their indifferent results, they fall back on excuses that have been used for centuries.

They argue that the obstacles to growth are so huge that you can't expect an easy solution. Or that you're going through a healing crisis and will eventually break through. Or that your negativity or pride or false views make you resistant to the truth. Or simply that you need to try harder.

This may seem like a heresy, but I think it is good to sometimes question the very idea of self-development. Is it just an attempt to be someone other than who we are? Is the idea that we can constantly get better and better just a myth without foundation? There is plenty of evidence that things change, but is improvement just in the eye of the beholder? There is no doubt that, beautiful as they seem, self-development systems often make people very miserable and confused.

SELF-AWARENESS

There are many Western techniques and disciplines that value self-awareness. This is the ability to look at one's body and mind honestly and dispassionately. This is quite different from analysing oneself according to a system or trying to attain to an ideal.

Meditation, by enhancing self-awareness, can work well with physical disciplines such as yoga or sports where you attune yourself exactly to the reality of your body. It helps with artistic disciplines, where you seek inspiration and examine in detail your perception of the world. It can help with philosophic disciplines in which you ask yourself, "Who am I? What is it to be human?"

Awareness helps greatly in those pragmatic therapies that encourage you to see yourself, and your self-deceptions, just as they are. These are therapies that give primacy to the client's experience, rather than to ideological constructs. Quite simply, if you see clearly what's causing you pain, you can do something about it.

It's not surprising that many Western meditation teachers are also counsellors or psychologists. Their curiosity about how the mind works probably took them from one to the other. Both meditators and psychologists need a keen eye to look below the surface, and to distinguish fantasy from fact. Furthermore, a psychologist who is calm and self-aware is less likely to project his own emotional issues onto a client. Meditation and therapy can work beautifully together.

Finally, meditation helps enormously in the journey of your 'soul', in whatever way you understand this mysterious word. By gaining access to deeper states of consciousness, you see deeply into your moods, feelings, dreams, and intuitions. You enter the territory where your soul comes alive.

SUMMARY

A calm clear mind is enormously valuable. It de-stresses you rapidly, body and mind. It keeps your body healthy and helps it heal when it's sick. It helps you cope well with dramas and enjoy life more. You learn to focus and study better, and let the unnecessary mental clutter go rapidly.

You perform better at work, on stage or on the sports field. You think more clearly, and think laterally and creatively. You tolerate your own shortcomings and those of others more readily.

When meditation combines with disciplines that involve belief or hope, some caution is required. Meditation is frequently used to induce a hypnotic, obedient and uncritical state of mind that makes you vulnerable to manipulation.

Meditation blends perfectly with disciplines, skills and therapies that value self-awareness and have a certain rational curiosity about how the body and/or mind works. It will help you find your own truths and know yourself as an individual. I encourage you to try it out and see where it takes you.

Products and Services

To conclude this book, I'll give you an overview of Perth Meditation Centre, and the services it provides. If you would like more up-to-date information, you are welcome to contact us by phone, or to examine the website.

PMC is at 280 Hay St in Subiaco, Perth, just east of the cafe strip. It is a large office suite at the top rear of a two-story building. It is an attractive, well-lit space and surprisingly quiet, being distant from most streets and offices nearby.

At PMC, I run four terms of courses and workshops, starting in February, May, July and October each year. There is a choice of ten or eleven courses each term, of seven weeks duration. This is the main body of my work.

I also offer private consultations for people who can't come to courses, or who have personal requirements regarding meditation. I also see experienced meditators who want to get more out of their practice.

In the past, I've run about forty retreats of two- to seven-days duration. Unfortunately, I now find the logistics of organising retreats demands too much of my time. I lead retreats now only if someone else organises them.

OUTSIDE WORK

I also teach extensively outside PMC, by means of seminars, courses and workshops. I've specialised in doing short economical courses for corporations, universities and Government bodies that fit into their time constraints. I've also helped one large corporation set up regular daily meditation sessions for their workers.

I'm periodically invited to run workshops in country areas, which I am always willing to do. I feel a certain affinity with remote communities, having lived in one in the past. I know how hard it is for them to get teachers for anything. I always find a wonderful response in rural areas. I spent about three weeks out of Perth doing this kind of work last year.

BOOKS

I just can't leave my books alone. I am always rewriting them to keep them up to date with the way I teach. This book has undergone several metamorphoses. It first appeared as a 48-page booklet entitled *Light on Meditation* in 1989. Two years later I produced it as a full-sized book called *Do You Want to Meditate?*

That self-published edition sold well and caught the eye of Simon and Schuster Australia. They published the fully revised edition in 1993, called *Teach Yourself to Meditate* to distinguish it from the earlier edition. They followed this up with a further revision in 1998. I've now resumed the rights to this book.

Simon and Schuster sold the book to publishers in China, Israel and England. When I self-published my next book, *How Meditation Heals*, I also sold it directly to Piatkus Books, my English publishers. The new Australian edition is due in April 2003

Piatkus Books has now sold one or other of those two books to publishers in other countries. They are now available in the Spanish, Italian, Swedish and Dutch languages, as well as Chinese and Hebrew. The American editions of both books, revised once again, came out last year.

Nonetheless, the most difficult book I've ever written was my overview of Buddhism, *The Naked Buddha*. It was very hard to find the right tone. I wanted to avoid the respectful stuffiness that writers tend to fall into when talking of someone else's religion. I find it best to say when the emperor has no clothes, even if he's admirable in other respects. The first edition of *The Naked Buddha* came out in 1998, just before a book of the same title by an Eastern States nun.

THE 3 CD SET, *HOW TO MEDITATE*

For years, I've held a dim view of meditation tapes and CDs. I find people who use tapes rarely meditate well without them, or even with them. But I also know how useful guidance can be for beginners, so after 14 years of teaching, I decided to produce my own series, entitled *How to Meditate*. I tried to avoid the usual shortcomings with CDs by making them as comprehensive as possible.

I was fortunate to have a marvellous collaborator in my friend, Ross Bolleter, a Zen teacher, composer and musician, who acted as my sound manager and musical director throughout. The resulting product is the ideal companion to this book. If you use both the CDs and the book, you maximise your chances of becoming a good meditator.

The CD set is an entire meditation course, duplicating the program I follow when I teach classes. It is designed to teach the student how to meditate without the CDs. The first CD gives all the instructions for the ensuing meditations. The second and third CDs contain eight guided meditations drawn from this book, with very light musical accompaniment.

DISTANCE EDUCATION

I frequently get calls and letters from people in the Eastern States saying, "I'd love to learn meditation I but can't come to Perth. Can you recommend a teacher near me?" And I usually can't. The CDs, however, are very suitable for people like these. Nothing quite replaces a teacher in the flesh, but the CDs, in conjunction with this book, are the next best thing.

You also have the option of doing a personal correspondence course with me or one of my assistant teachers. The course involves your using the CDs and the book, and discussing your practice with me once a week by phone or email or regular mail. Four to six weeks is usually enough to get you well on the way.

MEDITATION TEACHER TRAINING

Recently, I've trained some thirty people to teach meditation, and I am amazed at how inventive they are. Meditation blends very naturally with other disciplines: health care, yoga, therapy, spirituality and so on. It is now being done in corporations, in aged care facilities, in schools, in living rooms and in one-to-one sessions. It really does what the Buddha says it does: it reduces suffering and increases well-being and happiness.

I find that my students most commonly 'lead' meditations rather than 'teach' it as an independent skill. It's easy to lead a guided meditation, and it's often more appropriate than attempting to 'teach'. It is a wonderful way of taking schoolchildren, or sick or stressed people, into a better state immediately, or of setting the tone for a group. Later in 2003, I will run a correspondence course in Meditation Teacher Training.

Books and CDs

Do you Want to Meditate?
Perth Meditation Centre, Western Australia, 2002
Fully revised 4th edition, 224 pages, $20 + $5 postage

The Naked Buddha
A demythologised Account of the Man and his Teaching
Perth Meditation Centre, Western Australia, 1999
2nd edition, 240 pages, $20 + $5 postage

Why Meditation is Good for your Health
Perth Meditation Centre, Western Australia, 2003
3rd edition due out in April. $20+$5 postage

How to Meditate
Perth Meditation Centre, Western Australia 2001
A 3-CD set, with sound and music by Ross Bolleter
$70 + $5 postage

The above can be paid for by cheque or credit card
and ordered from:

PERTH MEDITATION CENTRE
P O Box 1019, Subiaco WA 6008, Australia
Phone: 08 9381 4877
www.perthmeditationcentre.com.au